P9-EAO-584

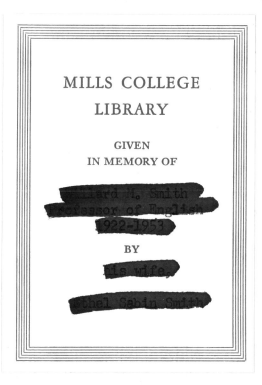

MILLS COLLEGE
LIBRARY

GIVEN
IN MEMORY OF

~~Willard M. Smith~~
~~Professor of English~~
~~1922-1953~~

BY

~~his wife,~~

~~Ethel Sabin Smith~~

SAY IT SAFELY
Legal Limits in Publishing, Radio, and Television

BOOKS BY PAUL P. ASHLEY

Cases on Business Law (Coauthor, 1929)
Essentials of Libel (1948)
You and Your Will: The Planning and Management of Your Estate (1975)
Say It Safely: Legal Limits in Publishing, Radio, and Television (First Edition, 1956; Fifth Edition, 1976)

Say It Safely

LEGAL LIMITS IN
PUBLISHING, RADIO,
AND TELEVISION

By Paul P. Ashley

In collaboration with Camden M. Hall

FIFTH EDITION

UNIVERSITY OF WASHINGTON PRESS · 1976
SEATTLE AND LONDON

The first edition of SAY IT SAFELY, published in 1956, replaced the author's
ESSENTIALS OF LIBEL: A HANDBOOK FOR JOURNALISTS, published in 1948.
Second edition, revised, 1959
Third edition, revised, 1966
Fourth edition, revised, 1969
Second printing, 1970
Third printing, 1972
Fifth edition, revised, 1976

Copyright © 1948, 1956, 1959, 1966, 1969, 1976
by the University of Washington Press
Printed in the United States of America

All rights reserved. No part of this publication may be reproduced or trans-
mitted in any form or by any means, electronic or mechanical, including
photocopy, recording, or any information storage or retrieval system, without permission in writing from the publisher.

345.73
A 826 s
1976

We have in this Country but one security. You may think that the Constitution is your security—it is nothing but a piece of paper. You may think that the statutes are your security—they are nothing but words in a book. You may think that an elaborate mechanism of government is your security—it is nothing at all, unless you have sound and uncorrupted public opinion to give life to your Constitution, *to give vitality to your statutes, to make efficient your government machinery.*

CHARLES EVANS HUGHES

Mills College Library
Withdrawn

MILLS COLLEGE
LIBRARY

Mills College Library
Withdrawn

PREFACE

My dear, dear lord
The purest treasure mortal times afford
Is spotless reputation; that away,
Men are but gilded loam or painted clay.

King Richard II
Act 1, Scene 1

Fifth Edition

THE calendar has been kind to *Say It Safely*. The third edition (1966) came shortly after the decision in *New York Times* v. *Sullivan*. A crystal ball made it possible to make conservatively vague predictions as to the course the law pertaining to qualified privilege might take. The fourth edition (1969) was able to predict with greater assurance. I know of no one whose fingers have been burned by relying on the forecasts, though I well realize that someone may have been hurt who did not tell me.

Now (1976) a cluster of court decisions makes it imperative to bring the varied progeny of *Times* v. *Sullivan* into focus (if that is possible) and to suggest, with prudent reservations, what the future holds for those who plead privilege in defense of alleged libel or violation of the right of privacy.

Of equal import is the restatement of the law of defamation and privacy tentatively approved by the American Law Institute in May 1975. This is the second restatement of those subjects; the first was adopted in 1938. So when working on this fifth edition of *Say It Safely* we have the benefit of the research and pronouncements of the Institute brought current after an interregnum of thirty-seven years. Indeed, the calendar has been kind.

During the days of writing the first edition (1955–56) I could not have envisaged the need of a chapter on obscenity and pornography. Today it is a must: Chapter 15. Another completely new chapter (19) is entitled "The Federal Constitution." I trust it will be helpful background for those who must refer to, and perhaps explain in laymens' language one or more of a parcel of constitutional provisions now often in the foreground.

An effort has been made to bring in adequate new material covering radio, television, and photography, with special emphasis on the problems of the political broadcast and on-the-spot radio and television reports. As before, in addition to offering a condensed presentation of the law of libel, the book discusses contempts of court, literary property, and the developing concept of right of privacy. Some chapters remain virtually unchanged. Others have been almost completely rewritten. Revisions have not been made merely for the sake of changing the wording of text which is still sound.

Say It Safely is designed for personnel of newspapers, publishers of magazines and books, radio and television broadcasters, the wire services and broadcasting networks, advertising agencies, and students looking toward a career in the field of mass communication. It will also answer practical questions for the public relations counsel of corporations, government, and professional and trade associations.

This book is a working tool designed for day-to-day use by all who write or process copy or speak over the airwaves. It is not a reference work that should repose in the library or morgue, or on the shelf across the room.

Nearly twenty years of using *Say It Safely* (plus eight years for its forerunner, *Essentials of Libel*) have demonstrated to thousands of craftsmen and executives the advantage of placing the book on each desk, convenient to reach and use.

It has been a rare pleasure to join with my colleague Camden M. Hall in the preparation of this fifth edition. If the cycle of juristic change follows the rhythm of the past, a sixth edition will become necessary by 1982. That edition, I hope, will be primarily Camden's responsibility.

In harmony with past practice, all author's royalties will go to University of Washington scholarship funds to be allocated to the School of Communications and the Law School.

January 1976   P.P.A.

CONTENTS

CONTENTS

SAY IT SAFELY
Legal Limits in Publishing, Radio, and Television

CHAPTER 1

THE ARENA

> *We should never so entirely avoid danger*
> *as to appear irresolute and cowardly.*
> *But, at the same time, we should avoid*
> *unnecessarily exposing ourselves to*
> *danger, than which nothing can be more*
> *foolish.*

> CICERO

LIBEL may be defined as any false statement, written or broadcast, which tends to (i) bring a person into public hatred, contempt, or ridicule; (ii) cause him to be shunned or avoided; or (iii) injure him in his business or occupation.

Not all libelous statements can be forbidden. Many must, should, or may be made. A witness must be free to speak the truth as he remembers it, though his memory may be frail and he falsely brings disgrace upon his neighbor. A judge must announce the facts he finds have been proved, though he, too, may err. The lawmaker must be able to debate freely; what he says must be in the public domain, uncensored and unchanged. Governmental affairs must be conducted under the searching light of criticism.

There is a continual contest within the law. Should communication of news and opinion be compressed into channels not harmful to individuals? Or should it be broadened for the public good? One aspect of the law of libel must protect persons. Another approach must recognize the people's need and right to know what goes on and to speak up in respect to public affairs. An equilibrium has not yet been reached, but rules are being forged.

I. History of Libel

Libel is not new in the law. The Papyrus of Hunefer shows the soul of that dignitary, then lately departed, pleading before the sun god, Osiris:

> I have not robbed;
> I have not slandered

and so on until he had pleaded not guilty to each of the forty-two offenses of which early Egyptian law took cognizance.

Moses commanded: "Neither shalt thou bear false witness against thy neighbor." The Far East punished slander. The Twelve Tables of Rome recognized defamation. Early Anglo-Saxon and Germanic laws took a serious view of insult by word or gesture. Punishments included excision of the tongue.

In England, a book on libel was written three hundred years ago. Under a French ordinance of the past century the publication of a libel was punished by whipping and, on a second offense, with death.

Lady Mary Wortley Montague remarked: "I am charmed with many points of the Turkish law. The proved authors of any notorious falsehood are burned on the forehead with a hot iron." If a South Pacific Islander hurts another person's body or his name, the *nanmarki,* the chief, must decide between them.

For a long time defamation has been universally recognized as a crime or as a civil wrong or as both. Redress for injury to reputation is one of the most cherished legal rights.

The rise of large newspapers during the nineteenth century and the development of radio and television during the twentieth have brought special legal problems. Capacity to inflict injury has become enormous. But daily deadlines and broadcast schedules make it difficult to take the precautions available to the publisher of a book or the writer of a speech. The current phenomenal growth of radio and television poses novel problems. A nationwide (occasionally, it may be said, worldwide) broadcast reaches millions of people. Injury may be done in many states. Should the law permit a dozen suits based on the same broadcast?

Despite its long history, the law of libel is still in a period of evaluation. It reflects a continuing attempt by society to reach a proper balance between the need of the individual for protection and the necessity for a free dissemination of news and fair comment in respect to public affairs and to public people.

RIGHT OF PRIVACY

Libel is an age-old risk. The year 1890 may be said to mark the birth of its kinsman, right of privacy. As will be shown in Chapter 12, whenever a publisher or broadcaster departs from the dictates of good taste and invades this newly come right of privacy, the right is given a chance to grow, step by step, by adverse court decision. If the trend continues, a day may come when violation of one's privacy is deemed a greater danger to publishers and broadcasters than is libel.

II. Hazards of Libel

Libel is an occupational hazard for all who communicate news, opinion, ideas, or pictures. Except as rarely granted by law, no publisher or broadcaster has prerogatives greater than those of the ordinary citizen.

Newspapers

Risk of libel cannot wholly be avoided by a newspaper that reports the news and dares to fight for honest government and suppression of crime. Deadlines and hot news demand fast handling and do not permit an exhaustive and scientific investigation of every facet of a story. Sometimes a paper's duty to its community requires exposure of corruption despite overt threat of suit by someone who thinks it will be impossible to prove in open court the facts which a reporter has unearthed, or even those which have become notorious.

Reports of crimes, trials, politics, public affairs, and many other stories involving defamation must be published. Neither reporters nor proofreaders are infallible; errors creep in. There is a day-to-day hazard that no newspaper worth reading or broadcaster worth hearing can completely escape. It is big in terms of dollars.

Radio and Television

The risks of libel when broadcasting spot news are about the same. Broadcasters face additional hazards inherent in the possibility of departure from script and in Federal Communications Commission regulations, particularly those pertaining to political broadcasts. These are considered in Chapters 13 and 14.

Though broadcasters do not editorialize and advocate for or against public measures as much as do newspapers, magazines, and books, the rules of fair comment and criticism reviewed in Chapter 8 are of consequence. For instance, some of the patter of a disc jockey can be justified only under the theory of fair comment and criticism. His remarks are not factual; they are but his opinion, and possibly his spontaneous opinion of the moment. When gossiping about private lives, some disc jockeys give the impression of stating supposed facts not meticulously documented as to accuracy. This tendency increases the hazards of their comments.

BOOKS AND MAGAZINES

With more time to be careful, the writers and publishers of books and magazines have an advantage over those under pressure of deadline and airtime schedules. They have a corollary burden—their libels may appear to be deliberate, hence less excusable.

THE PENALTY

Regardless of whether the laws of the state permit punitive damages (damages to punish the wrongdoer in addition to compensating the injured), juries do punish by large verdicts. Stable, long-established properties have been crippled as a result of one libelous comment.

Sometimes a jury is prejudiced against the publisher or his policies, or against the broadcaster. Perhaps more

7

frequently, the jury believes the publisher or broadcaster was wantonly careless, malicious, or so eager for circulation or listeners that he deliberately exploited false rumors of scandal.

Sometimes, when sued in a state court, the defendant may force removal to the federal court. Though bound by the law of the state in many aspects of libel as in other controversies, the federal court may be a better forum for the defendant when punitive or grossly excessive damages are sought—as is not unusual. Defendant's counsel will have recommendations as to strategy.

Where libel, privacy, or contempts of court may enter, every publisher and broadcaster is engaged in an extra-hazardous occupation.

III. The Theme

This manual is written for all writers, copyreaders, and telegraph, sports, women's, city, and other editors, authors, announcers, commentators, advertising personnel, proofreaders, printers, and the make-up crew who at one stage or another handle the copy which may contain dangerous matter. *They are the Fourth Estate.* Persons processing copy may be as much to blame when a libelous statement slips by unnoticed as is the excited cub reporter who telephones a story to the newsroom, or the advertising representative who brings in a defamatory political ad.

Most Libel Is Avoidable

Despite the dangers, all the news can be published or broadcast and a strong editorial policy maintained with little risk if basic legal principles are remembered and observed. Knowing how to recognize and then avoid libelous statements permits publication and broadcasting of stories and justified aggressive editorials which an uninformed person would have to kill because of fear of the unknown. Courage comes from confidence born of knowledge. Skilled mountaineers seldom fall; weekenders often do.

The purpose here is to state enough by way of rule or illustration to enable everyone to recognize the risk of libel—*always,* if he gathers the news and writes the story; *usually,* if he sees the copy but does not himself investigate the facts. The policy of all who engage in mass communication is presumed to be:

  (i) to write or pass copy or ads for publication or broadcast free of hazard;
 (ii) whenever dangerous copy is written or observed, to call attention to the risk of libel, violation of the right of privacy, or contempt of court, as the case may be.

Except for management (top brass, so to speak), the only question is—is this hazardous? If the answer is yes, the doubtful material should be stricken or so earmarked that it cannot escape the attention of those whose responsibility it is to accept or reject the risk of publishing or broadcasting dangerous statements.

RESPONSIBILITY OF FOURTH ESTATE

Nothing is more important to the maintenance of a free society than the preservation and enlargement of the right of the people to know what is happening in public affairs—and to criticize those who govern. The tendency of the executive branch of government is aggrandizement of power. The trend of the legislative is to impose ever increasing restrictions and to sidestep unpopular issues. A function of the judicial branch is to protect constitutional liberties.

Despite vexations and tribulations such as those inherent in the reporting of affairs criminal, the courts firmly uphold freedom of speech as assured in the Bill of Rights. In so doing, judges are sustaining their natural allies—the men and women of the Fourth Estate. Without the courts, the right to speak freely would wither. Without the searching scrutiny to which all branches of government are subjected by news media, the courts would not long survive as truly independent arbiters.

Though the courts have the final say, responsibility for preserving a relatively free form of government and the independence of the individual rests as much upon the Fourth Estate as upon the courts. Such is the high mission of all who communicate news and comment on public affairs.

This book is a tool to facilitate a more complete performance of that assignment. Because it prescribes Stop, Look, and Listen, in certain close situations the rules have been strictly construed against publishers and broadcasters. *In court, the interpretation should be more favorable than here indicated.*

CHAPTER 2

WHAT IS LIBEL?

Fore-warned, fore-armed.

CERVANTES

THE words "defame" and "defamation" include both libel and slander. If the defamation is by writing, picture (printed or televised), or cartoon, it is a libel. If it is by word of mouth, it is a slander. If over the airwaves, strictly speaking it is a slander. But because of the wide coverage—in contrast to mouth to ear—broadcasts are usually tested and redress given under the legal rules pertaining to printed publications. It should be assumed that when material goes on the air it is subject to the laws of libel, which are more severe than those relating to slander.

DEFINITIONS

Copy is defamatory if it tends to harm the reputation of any person by (i) exposing him to public aversion, (ii) lowering him in the estimation of his fellows, or (iii) deterring third persons from dealing with him. A corporation, partnership, club, or other association of individuals may be defamed as such.

Libel may stem from a story which exposes a person to hatred, contempt, ridicule, or obloquy. Words are libelous if they reflect unfavorably upon personal morality or integrity, or carry imputations which tend to damage financial standing. A story may be defamatory because it harms a person socially, although no reflection is cast upon his personal or business character. Even a criminal may be libeled, as by accusing an embezzler of kidnaping. A story reporting drunken driving may be libelous of a sober driver convicted only of speeding.

Still another definition may help make the meaning of libel as natural as the alphabet. California puts it:

> Libel is a *false and unprivileged* publication by writing, printing, picture, effigy, or other fixed representation to the eye, which exposes any person to hatred, contempt, ridicule, or obloquy, or which causes him to be shunned or avoided, or which has a tendency to injure him in his occupation.

The negation of "false and unprivileged" by proving truth or privilege, or both, is the most frequent defense.

Private vis-à-vis Public Persons

When it comes to recovering damages caused by defamation, public officials and public figures have burdens of proof not imposed on private individuals.

The term "public officials" includes those governmental employees (federal, state, and local) who have or appear to have substantial responsibility for or control over the conduct of governmental affairs. In addition the "position must be one which would invite public scrutiny of the person holding it, entirely apart from the scrutiny and discussion occasioned by the particular charges in controversy."

Though no precise definition has as yet been evolved by the courts, it may be said that a "public figure" is either (i) a person who has achieved such pervasive fame or notoriety that he has become a public figure for all contexts or (ii) a person who has voluntarily injected himself or is drawn into a particular public controversy and thereby becomes a public figure within the penumbra of that controversy.

For the purpose of applying the law of libel, all of the rest of us are private persons and so sometimes are public officials and public figures in relation to their strictly private affairs. A jury may be called upon to determine whether the aggrieved was defamed in regard to a private matter or his public capacity or activities.

When a plaintiff is found to be a public official or public figure and the story is in regard to his conduct as such, he may recover only if he can prove that (i) the publisher knew the statement was false and the plaintiff was the target or (ii) the publisher acted in reckless disregard of the truth. The consequence of (i) or (ii) is legal malice.

If plaintiff is a private person or the defamation is about a public official or public figure in respect to a *private* matter, plaintiff may recover damages if he can prove: (i) the publisher knew the statement was false and the plaintiff was the target, (ii) the publisher acted in reckless disregard of the truth, or (iii) the publisher was negligent in failing to ascertain that the statement was false and defamed plaintiff.

Elements sufficient to constitute negligence will be described in Chapter 4, "Intention, Negligence, and Mistake."

SAY IT SAFELY

Types of Civil Libel

1. A libel may consist of a *statement of fact*, that is to say, a report of a particular act, omission, or condition. A story which indicates that by act or omission a person has betrayed a trust, is guilty of dishonesty, fraud, or falsehood, has been cowardly, or cruel, has been profane, has been guilty of political corruption, has refused to pay his debts, or has been guilty of a crime, can be libelous. It may be libelous to report a condition of drunkenness, insanity, loathsome disease, or illegitimacy; or to say, for instance, that a person is a degenerate. Words that are in themselves innocent, but which, as used, injure another's business, property, profession, trade, or employment, may be actionable.

2. A libel can consist of a *statement of opinion* based on facts, actual or supposed.

> To say that a person is a hypocrite, faker, crook, sneak, criminal, a "Benedict Arnold," or otherwise to characterize him adversely may be libelous, whether or not the facts on which the remark is based are known to the reader.

The propriety of the opinion, in view of the provable facts, is a matter of judgment. In the heat of a campaign or crusade certain adjectives and epithets may seem proper enough. Later, calmly viewing all of the facts, a judge or jury may hold the words defamatory.

3. An *indirect statement or imputation* can be libelous if susceptible of a defamatory interpretation. Words written in jest may be read as libelous. Satire, irony, figure of speech, and innuendo may be defamatory, though not so intended.

An insinuation might be as actionable as a positive assertion, if the meaning is plain. Allusion, irony, and questions are within the bar if the defamatory inference is inherent. As a New York court put it:

> A man cannot libel another, by the publication of language, the meaning and damaging effect of which is clear to all men, and where the identity of the person meant cannot be doubted, and then escape liability through the use of a question mark.

4. *Error in identification.* A story otherwise true may become libelous because the subject is inaccurately identified, whether by error in name, address, picture, occupation, or other identifying characteristic. (Elaborated in Chapter 4.)

DISPARAGEMENT OF PROPERTY—SLANDER OF TITLE— TRADE LIBEL

A story disparaging another's property (whether land, buildings, chattels, or intangible things, such as a copyright), under such circumstances that it should have been foreseen that a purchaser or lessee of the property might be influenced adversely, may give rise to a cause of action in favor of the owner for the resulting pecuniary loss.

ILLUSTRATIONS

1. Published or broadcast in good faith, a story says that many titles in Grey Acre Subdivision are defective. That is not true. The title to the property has been disparaged, slandered. Plaintiff Jones, the owner, proves that sales were lost. Unless the story is privileged, Jones is entitled to damages.

2. The women's page or morning broadcast says a particular method of canning renders food unwholesome. Charles is a canner. His advertising and labels show he

used that method. There has been a trade libel. His business falls off. The broadcaster or publisher may be forced to prove the truth of the assertion.

Statements of this sort usually differ from a true libel which reflects on the character of the owner or operator, as when a boarding house is called a brothel. NBC learned the hard way that if a trade libel goes beyond disparagement and imparts fraud or deceit it becomes actionable without proof of special damage. During a telecast one of the performers displayed to his audience an object purporting to be a package of plaintiff's product, "Ezoons." He said: "Ezoons is full of all kinds of habitforming drugs. Nothing short of hospital care will make you stop taking Ezoons. You'll feel like a rundown hound dog and lose weight." This was a libel per se of the corporate manufacturer.

With increasing pressures to find buyers, some vendors are yielding to the temptation to defame a competitor's product. Under a headline "Rumors are Flying," it is reported that more companies are waging war on hearsay. These vendettas do not often involve media, although they may do so if the rumors are reflected in ads or news releases. Mention is made here merely to alert publishers to the possibility of an unlikely impact.

CHARITIES

A charitable corporation or association can be libeled. It is dependent upon public support. Defamatory statements which tend to lower it in public esteem may be actionable, subject of course to the usual defenses. To say falsely that a hospital is afflicted with streptococcus infection might be libel per se. On the other hand, large charitable operations

publication of the libel. It is of value to the distributor of
gazines and newspapers, the bookseller, and anyone
who can establish that:

(i) he disseminated the work without knowing that it
contained a libel; and
(ii) there was nothing in the work or in the circumstances which ought to have led him to suppose that
it contained a libel; and
ii) his lack of knowledge of the libel was not due to
negligence on his part.

efense may not be relied upon by printers—not even
shops printing small items. It does not shield anyone
sition to exercise judgment or discretion in respect to
t.

BY WILL

here filing of the will of a decedent with the clerk of
e court may or may not afford sufficient privilege to
justify republication of a libel contained in the
tial publication takes place when the will is filed.

ve nothing to my grandson Joe because
as a draft dodger and stole automobiles."

jurisdictions the estate would be responsible for
In others not. Do not quote libels from a will
ur attorney advises that the repetition is privi-

OFFICE

ibility of being excluded from the mails should
rely forgotten. The postman is one channel of

are quasi-public institutions, subject to comment and criticism, within the provable facts or those made privileged at
official public hearings.

CRIMINAL AND SEDITIOUS LIBEL

Defamations tend to disturb the peace. They make men
fighting mad. Thus, the state, as custodian of the peace, is
interested. A libel may be a crime in addition to giving rise
to a civil action in favor of the person defamed. Loosely defined, a criminal libel is a malicious or wanton publication
of defamatory statements or pictures. In contrast to civil
libel, truth cannot be relied upon as a defense against an accusation of criminal libel.

Defamation of the dead may be a criminal libel but does
not ordinarily give rise to a civil action. No further reference will be made to criminal libel; if the publisher avoids
flagrant civil libel, he will be safe from criminal charges.
Nor will seditious libel, which tends toward treason, be
touched upon.

MEANING OF WORDS

In testing for libel, the meaning of language is not limited
to orthodox dictionary definition. It hinges also upon the
temper of the times, colloquialisms, connotations, previous
and subsequent articles or broadcasts, and matters of common knowledge in the circulation or listening area.

Meaning reflects the whole picture in relation to day and
place of publication or broadcast and probably day and
place of trial should a suit be brought. Context enters into
meaning. It must be remembered that the words used will

be read or heard in the framework of public knowledge and common meaning. A judge or jury may not follow Mr. Webster.

> ILLUSTRATION
> To say that Joe Doakes, the gifted photographer, was having a hilarious time after five highballs would not, under most circumstances, be libelous of Joe. But to say that Joseph H. Doakes was enjoying similar festivities might be a libel per se if the reader or listener might reasonably conclude the reference to be to the Reverend Joseph H. Doakes, the eminent pastor of the First Baptist Church.

Subconsciously, emotion may influence the judicial mind. His Honor may be against air media generally because of the ads which interrupt his favorite television broadcast. Or he may be irked for years because of newspaper editorials condemning the judiciary for soft sentences in criminal cases.

I DID NOT MEAN TO

"I did not mean it that way" may not help. If some readers can naturally and reasonably understand a story to be defamatory, then it may be.

Standing alone, the statement "Smith got rich fast" would not imply corruption. But the assertion "Smith got rich fast while he was a tax collector" or the words "got rich fast" used in a context where it is implicit that Smith is or was the tax collector might well be libelous per se.

Interpretation is always in relation to time, place, and circumstances. Presently it may be libelous to call a man a Communist. But that was not necessarily so while Russia was our ally. The time may again come when it is not so.

Judges will not strip words to their
and ignore unfavorable implications. T
interpret pictures and cartoons in the
inoffensive sense in order to hold the

"PUBLISHER," "MEDIA," "BROADCAS

Unless the defamation is "publish
at least one third person, there is
hence no libel. The words are in
that when used in this book "publi
"publication" are words of art. Pu
communicates orally or visually
printing, drawings, photographs
statue for example—which conv
lisher" so defined, "publishin
clude all written, printed, oral,

"Media" means the custom
papers, radio, magazines, and
trade custom, and the courts
"broadcast" and "broadcaste
visual broadcasts, and they a

Unless the context requi
"copy," "reporter," "writer
both publication and broad
herein, it does not matter v
or is put on the air.

INNOCENT DISSEMINATI

Publication means
the libel. Innocent diss
persons who, innocent

communication. His regulations are to the effect that "any libelous, scurrilous, defamatory, or threatening language" will be excluded from the mails if it appears on the outside wrapper or envelope. Headlines may be readable, for instance, through a transparent wrapper. Postal regulations also limit the distribution of obscene material (Chapter 15).

CHAPTER 3

KEEP AWAY FROM
LIBEL PER SE

A man defames his neighbor at his peril.

POLLOCK

THE term "per se" means "by or in itself." When the defamation is evident from the article itself, without reference to an outside source, it is called a libel per se.

A libel per se is in itself a sufficient basis for a cause of action. Except as required by constitutional limitations (later discussed), plaintiff need not allege or prove he suffered actual dollar damage. In some states punitive damages (damages to punish defendant) are also allowed. The consequence is that the publisher or broadcaster must prove truth, or show privilege or other sufficient defense. The plaintiff is not required to prove the falsity. These are the dangerous libels.

In sharp contrast to libel per se, in unusual circumstances the most innocent-sounding copy may be defamatory. Suppose a story in print or over the air tells of the fine pitching of Jim Good at Saturday's sand-lot game. It should have said "Friday." If Jim is a leader in a church that makes Saturday the Sabbath, and forbids sports on a holy day, Jim may be libeled. But this is not a libel per se; lawyers often call it a libel per quod. Jim must demonstrate the defamation and prove that he suffered special harm.

These mild libels are difficult to recognize when editing script and reading copy or proof. They are not often important. Almost always a correction will cure the ill.

Except when management is evaluating risk, it should be assumed that anything which appears to be libelous may be libelous per se. If the publisher believes a story is of public importance, he may decide that although apparently defamatory, the statement is not a libel per se and may be broadcast or published because (even though libelous) it seems unlikely the plaintiff could prove he had suffered damage. Alternatively, it may be decided that despite the probability of a suit based on a libel per se where truth is the only real defense, the story should be told as a public duty.

The definitions of defamatory copy and pictures and all of the descriptions of types of civil libel found in Chapter 2 should be used as the measure of libel per se.

EXPRESSIONS LIBELOUS PER SE

Here classified are over two hundred specific expressions typical of those which may be held to be libelous per se. Connotation and context may control meaning. "It was a *gay* party of third graders, with ice cream and balloons." "He was drinking with two other *gays* at the tavern." Before words or expressions of the sort which follow are published, they should be submitted to management for decision.

Affiliations
  atheist
  Communist
  Fascist
  Ku Klux Klan
  Nazi
  nudist
  subversive groups
  any organization which, at the moment, is opprobri-
    ous
Attorneys
  ambulance chaser
  betrayed client
  hypocrite and altered records
  lacks requisite qualifications to practice
  pettifogging shyster
  shady
  shyster or shysterism
  tricky and dishonest
  unprofessional conduct
Authors and journalists
  attacks sanctity of home and desecrates memory of
    the dead
  defender of degenerates for hire
  humbug and fraud
  plagiarist
  rewrote another's work
Business establishments—corporations
  adulteration of products
  advertisement fraudulent
  complicity in swindle
  dirty products

driven out competitors and mercilessly robbed the
  people
false weights used
financially weak
fraud, a
hot, dirty, and poorly ventilated
precarious existence, not able to meet its financial
  obligations
price wrecker
racketeering methods
refuses to pay debts
swindle
unpaid claims
wares worthless
Businessmen
  bankrupt
  blackmail
  crook
  defrauding government
  evading payment of a debt
  false representations
  false weights used
  fraud
  gouged money
  sharp dealing
  short in accounts
Candidates, officeholders, politicians
  bribes or is bribed
  buys votes
  campaign of abuse and slander
  "Communist-line paper" supports him
  corrupt

deadbeat running for office for money
debauched the electorate with liquor
defaulter and bad moral character
dishonest treasury raid
falsifier of public documents
fawning sycophant
filching money from public
grafter
grossest dereliction of duty, if not crime
groveling office seeker
judge was a peril to children and sympathetic with
  criminals
paid dollars for office
partner of notorious criminal
perjurer
pockets public funds
received dollars for offices
reprehensible means used in campaign
scoundrel
sells his influence
sold out to the monopoly
solicited slush funds
stuffed the ballot box
superintendent of an institution permitted vile and
  immoral conditions
swindler

Clergymen
conduct unbecoming a married man and minister
curses, drinks, gambles
disgraceful conduct
intimate with choir leader
trouble with women

    unmannerly, discourteous, and ignorant
    unprincipled
Crimes
    any words imputing a crime regarded by the public
        as involving moral turpitude (petty misdemean-
        ors, such as overtime parking or jaywalking, are ex-
        cepted)
    connivance with crime
    consort with criminals
    extortion
    illegal
    unlawful
Disease
    any loathsome disease
    any acute mental disorder
    venereal diseases
Doctors or dentists
    abortionist
    advertising specialist
    caused death by reckless treatment
    charlatan
    drug addict
    faker
    fee exorbitant and operation unnecessary
    malpractice
    neglected patient
    quack
    unprofessional conduct
    used improper instruments
Domestic difficulties
    another wife elsewhere
    divorce action instituted (i.e., when none had been)

having wife trouble

philanderer

reference to a controversy concerning custody of
children as though divorce suit is pending, when
actually completed and a parent mentioned in story
has remarried

Drunkenness or liquor

aiding moonshiners

booze hound

drunkard

kept booze for unlawful purposes

toper

Honesty (see also *Reputation*)

amoral

con man

crook

dishonesty

dishonorable

fraud

guilty of falsehood

liar

rogue (not "a jolly rogue")

shameful

unreliable and does not meet his obligations

unworthy of credit

Hotels, apartments, and boarding houses

brothel

disorderly house

gambling house

vice den

Labor and management

company put on unfair list

company violated its union contract

employer falsified facts to workers and the public
racketeers
scab (sometimes)
strikebreaker and foe of labor
union officials corrupt

Morality
adulterer
affinity
bigamist
fornicator
gay (depends on context)
homosexual or a queer
illicit relations
infidelity
libertine
lovemate
mistress
moral delinquency
moral obliquity
promiscuous lovemaker
prostitute and equivalent terms
queer (depends on context)
seducer
unmarried mother
unchastity
villain
whore

Obituaries (person not dead)
death in discreditable circumstances
suicide, or other disgraceful cause

Officeholders (see Candidates, etc.)

Patriotism
anarchist

flag, called it a dirty rag
red-tinted agitator
secret foreign agent
seditious agitator
spreader of distrust, discontent, and sedition
traitor
Politicians (see *Candidates,* etc.)
Reputation (see also *Honesty*)
deadbeat
disreputable
gambler
horse thief
hypocrite
illegitimate
jumped his board bill
low grade creature of crass ignorance and stupid
egotism
no honorable reason for . . .
poltroon
rascal
skunk
suicide attempted
venality
vile and slanderous tongue
wastrel
Sanity
fit to be sent to asylum
just a little daft
unsafe to be at large
unsound mind
Teachers
double-talk by school official
ignoramus

incompetent
intemperate
shameless skulduggery
unfit to be on faculty
unladylike conduct, unfit to teach school
This and that
blasphemy, guilty of
community cannot despise him more
deprived of ordinances of the church
ejected by police (the reference being to a reputable
  citizen)
informer
infringed a patent
insulted females
juror agreed to determine verdict by lot
juror agreed to determine verdict by game of
  checkers
jurors did injustice to oaths
libelous journalist
publisher of a libel
suicide, in reference to a living person
uses cloak of religion for unworthy purposes

All of the foregoing words and expressions should be considered libelous per se. However, *as a matter of defense,* under special circumstances not to be relied upon in advance, certain of them may be held not libelous per se. For instance, a state supreme court held it not libelous per se to call a candidate a liar when referring only to his campaign ads and not to him as a person. The judges slapped the wrists of the writer and the editor by remarking that the word is "unbecoming of a reputable newspaper."

RECAPITULATION

Specific false expressions such as those just listed (all included in the types of libel described in Chapter 2) may be reclassified into four kinds of libel per se:

1. Accusations or imputations of crime.
2. Statements or insinuations of insanity or of loathsome or contagious disease.
3. Assertions of want of capacity to conduct one's business or profession.
4. Any expression which tends to bring public hatred, contempt, or ridicule.

SINISTER CONDUCT INFERRED

The fact that a matter is viewed as newsworthy supports the inference that something of special importance is being communicated. The classic example is that of the mate who truthfully wrote in the ship's log: "Captain sober today." It is a libel per se to accuse a captain of drunkenness when aboard ship.

ARSENIC AND OLD LACE

A Boston newspaper ran an article stating that the hospital suspected that Mary Perry's husband (whose death was being probed) suffered from chronic arsenic poisoning. The writer embellished this provable fact, in itself not particularly significant, by adding: (i) decedent's brother had died approximately a month later after having spent two days "here" for the funeral, (ii) Mary's mother had died after she came to live with her daughter and her remains were cremated, and (iii) decedent was Mary's second husband.

Remarks (i), (ii), and (iii) are innocent whether read severally or collectively. But why include them in a story saying that the autopsy "disclosed that 500 times the usual amount of arsenic was in his hair"?

The court of appeals answered in language most elegant:

> Taking the article as a whole we believe it would be only natural for readers to assume that they were being furnished with something more than necrology, or trivia concerning the relict of a routinely posted cadaver, and that they could well conclude that the plaintiff was suspected of having engaged in highly sinister conduct.

The lesson is that the very act of sensationalizing an otherwise innocent story may make it a libel per se.

CHAPTER 4

INTENTION, NEGLIGENCE, AND MISTAKE

Hell is paved with good intentions.

SAMUEL JOHNSON

MOST libel actions stem from careless research, reporting, or writing or from loose treatment in the course of editing, printing, or broadcasting—including departures from script. Many a libel comes from what may be termed unimaginative handling of a routine story, i.e., no one noticed that, while superficially innocent of libel, the story was actually libelous per se. *Attempts to build a story out of little or nothing involve disproportionate risks.*

GOOD INTENTIONS

If the words are susceptible to a defamatory meaning, the copy or script may be libelous despite the most innocent of motives. The publisher or broadcaster may be liable even though:

(i) the writer carefully gathered data and believed them to be true;

(ii) he did not intend the story to be read in a defamatory sense;

(iii) he did not realize that it could be so understood;

(iv) the libel was caused by typographical error or a slip of the tongue;

(v) the author thought the words or pictures were fictional—not referring to anyone; but there were people within the descriptions;

(vi) all was in jest—no harm intended;

(vii) no copyreader, continuity editor, proofreader, or anyone else suspected defamation.

If even a minority of readers, listeners, or viewers could reasonably interpret the story or picture as defamatory, the court or jury may so construe it. When words are ambiguous, the jury may be allowed to consider testimony of hearers or readers as to how they understood them. That gives plaintiff's friends a golden opportunity.

Good faith is of course a defensive aid. In contrast, if anyone preparing, passing upon, or handling copy has been negligent in failing to observe discernible error, the defendants in the libel case have two strikes against them.

HEADLINES

Defamatory headlines may or may not be cured by explanations in the story. The courts realize that frequently the reader catches the headlines, then reads the article itself so hastily that he fails to grasp fine distinctions.

CAUTION
Because of their brevity, headlines may be ambiguous. When the story itself is close to being dangerous, the headlines must be watched with special care.

Misuse of headlines occurs most frequently in connection with reports of criminal investigations. "Murderer Apprehended," "Kidnaper Caught," "Sheriff Nabs Thief," and the like may be libelous though followed (it might be said because followed) by a story explicitly stating that the suspect has only been arrested or charged and stoutly maintains his innocence.

ILLUSTRATIONS

1. One newspaper suffered a large verdict for its headline, "Spy Caught." A competitive paper escaped liability because its headline was, "Arrested Aboard Ship as Spy."

2. A headline saying, "Doctor Kills Child," was followed by a story of an auto accident in which the doctor driver was perhaps negligent but certainly not deliberately reckless. The headline misled. It connoted intent or unprofessional conduct.

3. The headline was "Babies for Sale . . . Trade of Child Told." The tagline read, "Tomorrow—Blackmail by Franklin." The body of the article accurately recited the facts concerning the adoption in question. The publisher contended that the headline and tagline cannot be considered apart from the context in which they were used. The Supreme Court of Nevada answered: "This is not so . . . the public frequently reads only the headlines."

A wire service is not liable for headlines added by a newspaper.

LEAD PARAGRAPHS

The headline may be followed by a lead paragraph—either in print or by the broadcaster who assures us that he will be back on the air after an important message. His introduction *before* the station break is of course vitalized to hold the listener during the recital of the merits of the sponsor's product.

The headline plus a well written lead paragraph digests the whole story. Many read or hear no further. So appealing arguments can be made to the court to the effect that if a defamation lurks in the leads, the aggrieved may not be bound by the general rule that a story must be considered as a whole. The closing paragraphs may round out the specifics and show that plaintiff was not accused of anything wrong. But mere perusal of the headlines and lead paragraphs (or listening only to the preliminary enticements of the broadcast—"Rapist apprehended; details after message from sponsor") may leave quite a different impression.

So the careful editor will make sure the headlines and first sentences do not carry libel without also a forecast of a sufficient explanation.

IDENTIFICATION

Although the writer and all others passing upon copy or script honestly believe the reference is applicable only to a certain person, there is not sufficient excuse if, in fact, the public may reasonably think the story applies to another person. The test is not whom the story intends to name but who a part of the audience may reasonably think is named—"not who is meant but who is hit," as one court put it.

ILLUSTRATIONS

Acquaintances might be able to identify an unnamed subject from:

1. "Veteran's wife says he beat her and year-old triplets."

2. "Mr. Rothschild, the bank's president, believes that

a newly employed watchman is implicated in the robbery."

3. A story, libelous per se, was about Hugh Cameron. There were two Hugh Camerons in the vicinity. The picture of the innocent Cameron was published. That Hugh had a huge cause of action.

A piece in the *Chicago Tribune* told of a vice raid. Dolores Reising, fifty-seven, alias Eve Spiro and Eve John, was named as the suspected keeper of the apartment. Plaintiff was twenty-seven years of age. She resided in an apartment below the one raided. Coincidentally, her maiden name had been Eve Spiro and her name at the time, although she was divorced, was Eve John. She was in no way involved in the raid or the immoral activities of her landlady. The Supreme Court of Illinois held that the story was not "of and concerning" the twenty-seven-year-old; she was not libeled.

Libelous statements were published about the conduct of a corporation, but no officer was mentioned. The president sued. He proved it was well known he controlled the corporation; ergo, the townsfolk understood that he had been charged with the nefarious acts. He was allowed recovery without proof of special damage. *Query:* Would not the result have been the same if the public had thought him to be the boss even though he was a mere figurehead in the corporate affairs?

A telecast sponsored by the Better Business Bureau defamed the "Day and Night Television Service." The partners brought suit although neither had been named and one was a silent partner, not acting in the business. The libel of the trade name was held a libel of the two partners, either of whom was entitled to maintain the successful action against the broadcasting company.

When a person is identified by address, vocation, hobby (such as archery), relatives, or other data, the indicia, if in error, may make the story libelous. Suppose a story says that Bill Brown, former football star, was arrested for drunken driving. The name was correct, but the deputy sheriff was in error as to football stardom. The story libels the football star of that name.

> CAUTION
> If a coined name is used, make sure it will not fit some living person or that it is obviously a "John Doe" type of name, not applicable to anyone in particular.

The persons named must be sufficiently identified. Otherwise someone else of that name may be able to state a cause of action. A defamatory statement names Richard Roe of Milwaukee, without further identification. Three Richard Roes live in that city. Two of them might be in a position to state a cause of action for a libel even though the story is true as to the third.

It should not be assumed that similarity in names means identity of persons.

LIBEL BY REFERENCE TO A CLASS

An individual may be defamed by words which disparage a small group of which he is a member, as by a statement that "the members of the school board are corrupt." Hence, fine discrimination must be exercised when deciding whether a reference to a small body of people (or to an unnamed member or members thereof) identifies particular persons.

The size of the group is a critical, but not necessarily the controlling, factor. Obviously a reference to "a corrupt Congressman" or to "corrupt Congressmen" does not in itself identify anyone in that huge body. But a libelous statement referring to the congressional delegation from a named state, particularly a small state, might be actionable by some or all of those congressmen.

ILLUSTRATION
Assume a board of twelve city councilmen and, in the same area, a board of three county commissioners. Accusations of graft in city and county government may require different treatments.

GROUP LIBEL

Statutory libel of the group itself is in sharp contrast to libel of an individual by reference to his group. An occasional law prohibits any publication or broadcast which, for instance, "would expose citizens of any race, creed, or color to contempt, derision, or obloquy." Such restrictions are primarily penal.

SUCCESSIVE STORIES

In a succession of stories, a person may be libeled by a story in which he is not named and from which story (if read alone) he cannot be identified, if he is named or identified in a previous or subsequent story. Hence, all of a series must be read together for the purpose of determining possible libel and identification.

ILLUSTRATION
Anxious to acquire funds to finance law school, two students evolved an elaborate abduction-robbery scheme to plunder a liquor store. Plans went awry. Harry was caught hiding under burlap sacks in the store. He con-

fessed, giving details other than the identity of his accomplice. The case was novel, and open and shut as to Harry. Media ran stories sufficient to convince readers of the guilt of both.

Later David was charged. If (i) the second series of stories names David in contrast to "student held," and (ii) David pleads not guilty and is acquitted, the series of stories defames a legally innocent aspirant to the bar.

MALICE FROM CARELESSNESS

In the eyes of the jury carelessness merges into recklessness. They both feed a charge of malice. For practical purposes it is not necessary here to delve into what constitutes malice—actual and constructive. Suffice it to say that if the tone of a story or comment or the circumstances of publication or broadcast indicate malice toward the plaintiff, the jury will be slow to believe the defenses and might be lavish in the verdict.

A pungent definition is that as an ingredient of an action for libel, "malice signifies nothing more than a wrongful act done intentionally, without just cause or excuse."

NEGLIGENT MISTAKE

Occasionally a publisher is threatened with litigation bottomed on the negligent publication of an untrue statement which is *not* libelous. Most of the reported cases which originate in the news columns stem from false reports of death, bringing anxiety to those who believe themselves bereaved. Some decisions recognize a "duty if one speaks at all," to give correct information.

Errors in ads are more apt to be false figures than a misstatement of text. The publisher announced "a bargain at

$9.95." The copy submitted by the advertiser read "$29.95." Sometimes a correction pacifies the advertiser and his customers; sometimes not. A directive from general management to the store managers of one of the largest national outlets is essentially: "Store go ahead and sell at the advertised price; if media are responsible for incorrect price, description, etc., we will pass loss on sales back to the newspaper or station." Of course, each instance must be handled in its own framework.

An item to remember: If the error is bad enough, the store's customers could not be misled. Assume, for instance, the picture of a mink stole normally selling for, say, $850. The copy carried a bargain price of $695. If the printed ad or broadcast puts the price at $395, the advertising department is in trouble. The ladies will flock in to buy the stole at $395. But if the mistake is so gross that no sensible person should be misled, the publisher is in an embarrassing but not so serious situation. A published price of $19.95 for that stole should alert everyone to the fact that a mistake has been made. In contrast, if the mistake were a reduction to $395, the store might well feel obligated to honor its ad, with consequent damages assessable to the publisher in addition to the running of a corrected ad.

A suit based on negligent mistake with no allegation of libel seldom finds its way to a supreme court. Actual damage resulting from non-libelous news stories is rare and hard to prove. Certainly, however, a justified complaint concerning a negligent news story gives the cue for a prompt and clear correction, if feasible, in a manner desired by the persons who claim injury.

CHAPTER 5

QUOTATIONS AND ADS

Tale-bearers are as bad as the tale-makers.

SHERIDAN

PUBLISHERS and broadcasters may not repeat false and defamatory matter and escape liability with the plea that they were but quoting a source deemed authentic or passing along current news already published or on the air. They are not saved by naming the author or origin, or even by accompanying the defamation with an expression of disbelief.

QUOTATIONS—IN GENERAL

Except in a relatively few situations (there is occasional statutory relief where the publisher has no reason to know of the defamation) publishers may be held liable for unprivileged quotations, whether in the news columns, commentaries, editorials, or ads. They may be responsible for what their columnists and commentators say and their cartoonists depict, despite editorial disavowal of sponsorship and disagreement with the statements made. A gossip column,

43

feeding on tips, with trivial news value is particularly vulnerable.

Truth, privilege, fair comment as recently construed by constitutional interpretations, and other defenses are of course available. But the defense of truth requires more than merely proving that the quoted statement was made by someone else. The jury must be satisfied that the defamatory assertions are substantially correct.

ILLUSTRATION

At a community club meeting an indignant citizen asserted that a certain officeholder "pockets public funds." This was repeated by the press and over the air. Libel suits ensued. A host of witnesses testified that those very words had been used. Such testimony does not prove truth. The occasion being unprivileged, the defendants must convince each juror that plaintiff did pocket public funds. (*Part V of Chapter 7 considers the privilege attendant upon public meetings.*)

If the source of the story is such that some privilege may attach, that source should be identified, as by name and office. The loose expression "high officials state" is a weak foundation upon which to build a defense of privilege. Reference to a proper specific source shows authenticity and the propriety of relying upon that source.

ILLUSTRATION

For cause of death, quote "J. B. Ded, King County Coroner," if possible, rather than someone in another department. If the story has to do with an investigation of graft or faulty construction in the erection of the new city hall, quote the Mayor or head of the Board of Public Works, not a councilman, unless he has special responsibilities or is known to be well informed.

The stock phrases, "it is alleged," "it is reported," "police say," and so on are meaningless so far as liability for defamation is concerned unless the story is actually privileged.

It distills almost to this: In the absence of privilege, one who repeats another's defamatory remarks is legally responsible unless he has available defenses which would shield him were he the author.

While the publisher should use quotation marks when appropriate, he should be sensitive to their possible misuse. The careless use of quotation marks may lend the quoted word or expression an inverted meaning or a meaning opposite to that of the words themselves—or it may give undue or sarcastic emphasis to certain words and thus give rise to a defamatory interpretation.

ADVERTISEMENTS

When passing upon advertising copy and script, apply the general rules pertaining to libel. In addition, the possibility of disparaging (libeling) the property or business of a third party must be kept in mind (see Chapter 2, Trade Libel). Unnamed individuals may be identified by reference to their business or trade name. The ad that appears on the screen in a telecast should be scrutinized, as well as the script that the announcer will read.

An advertiser is permitted to push his own merchandise or services until he approaches the border lines of fraud and misrepresentation. However, his promotions must be by way of praise of his own product, not by unfair disparagement of his competitor.

STATUTES

In some states there are statutes imposing artificial, in contrast to common law, restrictions upon advertising. Indeed, legislation of this sort is sometimes found in city ordinances with municipal, but not statewide, effect. Local counsel should be consulted in these matters.

Likewise, advertising must conform to postal and other governmental regulations—for instance, in respect to gambling.

We will shortly discuss product and service selling ads as contrasted with advocacy advertising which champions economic, social, or political measures.

ADS CONCERNING PUBLIC OFFICIALS

Compressed coverage of the privilege pertaining to ads concerning public officeholders and political candidates is included in this chapter only as an aid to quick reference. A study of Chapters 6, 7, and 8 is essential to an understanding of what is said here.

Paid public ads are within the privilege protecting those who—without malice—make factual errors when critizing the conduct of public officials or public figures. Were this not so, "editorial advertisements" would be discouraged and thus shut off an important outlet for the promulgation of information and ideas by persons who do not themselves have access to the press and the airwaves.

Following a like rule previously adopted by a number of states, in the *New York Times* case (1964) the Supreme Court of the United States held that constitutional guarantees prohibit "a public official from recovering damages for a defamatory falsehood *relating to his official conduct* unless he proves that the statement was made with actual malice—that is, with knowledge that it was false or with reckless disregard of whether it was false or not" (emphasis added). This decision has been extended to include public figures.

This sound rule may trap the unwary. It is not, for example, a license to print or broadcast any political ad concerning an officeholder. Perhaps responsible personnel do know of the falsity, and the circumstances are such that their knowledge will be imputed to the publisher. Or careless handling of copy may influence a judge or jury to find that there was a reckless disregard of whether or not the ad was false.

Note well the phrase "relating to his official conduct." A frequent vice of political advertising—particularly during campaigns—is to purport to expose the private life of the officeholder or otherwise attack him in respect to matters not related to his official conduct, fitness, or role as a public official.

ADS CONCERNING CANDIDATES OR PUBLIC FIGURES

The privilege described in the preceding paragraphs applies to ads attacking officeholders. Public policy requires a like latitude regarding the qualifications of a candidate for public office and persons who are clearly "public figures." Such has become or is becoming prevailing law.

However, *it is still prudent to assume the publisher may be put to the burden of proving the substantial truth of libelous assertions concerning a candidate not yet in office or a public figure.* His *personal* life may not affect his qualifications for the office he seeks or his civic activities. He may never have been an officeholder and made a record in public affairs. So there may be a tendency to descend to personal abuse.

47

PRACTICAL POLITICS

Not infrequently a campaign committee offers a libelous or a borderline ad with the assertion that "this has been approved by our attorney and he says it is safe." If the copy is plainly libelous per se, it should not be run or broadcast unless management is on a crusade, is confident the assertions are true or privileged, and knowingly assumes the risk.

If, however, there is some question as to whether it is safe, and the sponsors of the ad are responsible and solvent, a practical out is to suggest to the committee:

> You, of course, have confidence in your attorney. Our attorney is doubtful, but you have a greater factual background, and ours may be unduly apprehensive. If all members of your committee and their spouses will enter into an agreement to pay our expenses incident to trial and to indemnify us if any judgment should be entered against us, we will be glad to print or broadcast your ad.

Almost always this ends the matter and snuffs out criticism to the effect that the publisher or broadcaster is too timid or biased.

Political ads may be subject to statutory requirements touching identification of sponsors and related matters.

REFUSAL TO ACCEPT PRINTED ADVERTISING

The public has a strong interest in the operation of newspapers and magazines. However, the courts hold that publication is a private enterprise and that those who engage in it are free to deal with whomever they choose. Hence, any advertising may be refused unless the refusal furthers an illegal monopoly, conspiracy, or other unlawful purpose.

SAY IT SAFELY

protected when republishing what has been sent you from abroad, you should assume that you are not.

The greatest danger comes where the person libeled is a resident of your circulation or broadcast area. The story may place him three thousand miles from his accustomed abode as a participant in a disgraceful episode. But perchance he was quietly at home, wholly free from taint of wrong. The publisher might be held grossly negligent in failing to make energetic efforts to check the facts through local channels.

This red signal is so important that it is lighted again at the end of Chapter 17, "Danger Zones."

BIENNIAL REFRESHERS

Most political ads come in election years—perhaps biennially. Advertising personnel are not constantly faced with libel, as are reporters and the writers of editorials. The advertising staff may not be libel conscious, and ads can slip by which would be refused if read with discernment. A salesman who has been on the job for a year and a half—between elections—considers himself experienced, yet he may never have handled libelous copy. In fairness to advertising personnel, it is suggested that they are entitled to a refresher on libel before each hot campaign.

BILLING FOR ADS

Roughly worded follow-ups to advertisers who neglect to pay their bills may bring the business office afoul of the Post Office Department. It forbids any mailing which has on its outside "any language asking for payment of a bill, which by its manner or style of display is defamatory and reflects injuriously on the character of addressee." Some-

ADS ON THE AIR

Radio and television have broader responsibilities in respect to treating all alike when the interest of the public may be involved. Their discretion in refusing purely *commercial* advertising is as wide as that accorded other privately owned media. But because each uses an exclusive channel allocated and licensed under federal law, they have less discretion when the proffered ad is in connection with a political campaign or touches matters of public interest. Chapter 14 ("Political Broadcasts") and Part II of Chapter 13 ("Controversial Issues and the Fairness Doctrine") cover these areas.

The provisions of the Communications Act are such that the station has "no power of censorship over the material broadcast by a qualified candidate." Ordinary rules do not apply.

COMMERCIAL ADVERTISING VIS-À-VIS VIEWPOINT ADVERTISING

Most ads are designed to sell products or services. Commercial advertising is not a form of speech which the Constitution vigorously protects. Hence the conservative legal approach when passing on such a proffered ad must be that it enjoys no First Amendment (freedom of speech) protection.

However, media should not concede that *all* commercial advertising is devoid of First Amendment protection. Indeed, sometimes it is difficult to be dogmatic as to whether an ad is purely commercial or whether basically, at least in part, it is a protected publication, the advocacy or elucidation of public programs.

In contrast, there are ads devoted exclusively to the exposition of a point of view—political, social, or economic—as well as the ads of candidates for public office already discussed. Advertising designed not to sell something for someone's profit but to explain a theory affecting the public weal or to advocate support of a program affecting the public is within the principles pertaining to freedom of speech and of media.

A recent decision of the Supreme Court gives a vivid example of constitutionally protected speech even though it appears in a paid advertisement. A Virginia newspaper published the announcement of a New York concern that it would arrange to place women plagued with unwanted pregnancies in accredited New York hospitals or clinics where abortions were legal. There were no requirements as to residency. The editor of the paper was convicted of violating a Virginia statute making it a misdemeanor to thus encourage an abortion.

Reversing the Virginia courts the Supreme Court held them in error for assuming in effect that advertising, as such, was not entitled to First Amendment protection (Chapter 19). Freedom of speech is not stripped from what is said in paid publicity, by air or print.

Proffered advertising which contains within it possible libel or violation of privacy and which is not manifestly a public-interest advertisement (as the advertiser believes) should be carefully weighed in light of then current public issues, national and local. *If the balance tilts in favor of public interest, discretion should of course be used and virulent phrases deleted as would be done in any political ad.* Here, in passing, it should be mentioned that juristic attitude toward an ad may be influenced by the nature of the product. An ad extolling furniture or foods might be judged

quite differently from the standpoint of local regula[t] libel, or violation of privacy than would an ad contain[i] camouflaged offer for contraceptive devices or a theat[for a seemingly obscene show.

THE FANATICAL FRINGE

A few campaigns ago an ad was offered to some ne[pers soliciting readers to purchase books concerning nounced candidate for president of the United State[ferred to the candidate's inability to read, write, [without difficulty and consequent reliance on ghost[It accused him of financing the North Vietnamese a[horrendous activities.

The answer of the advertising department to th[of that fanatical copy is clear: "Thank you, no." It i[the utmost penumbra of the *New York Times* rul[tion.

The extreme tenor of some political attacks (s[that just cited) may justify a jury finding that the must have in fact entertained serious doubt as to t[the published material. When the averments of th[so inherently improbable that only a reckless m[have put them in circulation, the publisher may The virulence of an attack may make publicatio[disregard of truth.

THE WIRE SERVICES

It is obvious that a publisher cannot double[facet of every story and commentary which co[wire. A few statutes and decisions afford relie[you have positive advice from your attorney times an economy-minded credit department (or its dele-gate, a collection agency) uses postcards, particularly for classified ads. Occasionally, over-zealous collection efforts end in libel suits against the creditor.

CHAPTER 6

PRIVILEGE—WHO HAS IT?

The only security of all is in a free press. . . . No government ought to be without censors: and where the press is free no one ever will.

THOMAS JEFFERSON

THE broad term "privilege" includes both absolute privilege and qualified or conditional privilege. Publishers and broadcasters enjoy no absolute privilege. For them and for all who do not qualify as actors on a stage affording absolute privilege, the privilege is qualified or conditional. This chapter is devoted to the general nature of absolute and qualified or conditional privilege.

I. ABSOLUTE PRIVILEGE

Absolute privilege is strictly limited, both as to the persons whose utterances are protected and the occasions on which it may be invoked. It allows any statements, however erroneous and however damaging, about any person, with complete protection from accountability for the libelous utterance. It is a freedom conferred only when the rights of individuals to protection against libel must be subjugated to the common good, i.e., the individual's interest in his reputation must be sacrificed in order to permit the free functioning of the processes of government.

By-passing certain private occasions (husband-wife, priest-penitent, and a few others), the rule is that absolute privilege applies only in three general areas: (i) judicial proceedings, (ii) legislative proceedings, and (iii) the acts of important government officials, usually executives. *If statements absolutely privileged when uttered are repeated by others, the privilege becomes qualified or conditional.*

JUDICIAL PROCEEDINGS

A judge or other judicial officer, an attorney participating in a judicial proceeding, parties to litigation, witnesses, and jurors are all absolutely privileged to make false and defamatory statements during and as part of the trial, if they bear some relationship to the matter under consideration.

LEGISLATIVE PROCEEDINGS

A member of the Congress of the United States or of the legislature of any state or territory is absolutely privileged to say false and defamatory things in the performance of his legislative function. This privilege includes statements made on the floor of a legislative body and extends to the work of legislative committees engaged in investigation or other work authorized by the legislative body. It also extends to legislative aides who are engaged in the legislative process. It may not encompass newsletters to constituents or speeches made outside of legislative or committee proceedings.

In a lesser assembly (a town council, for instance) a member may enjoy the same privilege but it may be lost if he is malicious or if his remarks become irrelevant to the public matter then under consideration.

GOVERNMENT OFFICIALS

The president of the United States, the governor of any state or territory, the cabinet officers of the United States, the heads of important branches of the federal government, and corresponding officers of any state or major municipal or other government entity are absolutely privileged when making false and defamatory statements if (i) they are made in the course of executive proceedings in which the officer is acting, and (ii) they have some relation thereto.

ILLUSTRATIONS

1. The president of the borough of Queens submitted a report to the mayor which said that plaintiff's appraisals were based on "misinformation, ignorance, distortion and incompetence." Condemnation procedures were commanding public interest. Three months later, defendant made a copy of his report available for newsmen. It was publicized. The court held: (i) the borough president acted within the scope of his official duties. He had an absolute privilege when making the libelous statements contained in his report to the mayor. (ii) Release to the press was within the scope of his absolute privilege. The report covered a matter of public concern. Upon demand, he was obliged to release this public document.

2. A highway contractor complained because a member of the highway commission said he should be barred from bidding on future jobs and that certain actions of the contractor were "premeditated, malicious and done with intent to defraud" the government. The state-

ment was made at a meeting of the commission, with reporters present. The Supreme Court of New Mexico held that the commissioner was such an officer of the state as to be absolutely privileged if what he said had some relation to the executive proceeding in which he was participating.

3. In the course of a fracas concerning Japanese bonds, the superintendent of banks made libelous statements concerning plaintiff, formerly his attorney. They were repeated in the news reports. The Supreme Court of California held that the public statement made by the superintendent in defense of the policies of his department was in the exercise of an executive function and protected by an absolute privilege.

4. During discussion of the operation of the police department at a regularly scheduled meeting of the city council, a councilman stated that a deputy city marshal had "propositioned" a woman to whom he was issuing a traffic ticket. Finding that the remark had a reasonable relation to the subject of the meeting, the Supreme Court of Utah held the councilman protected by an absolute privilege.

5. In contrast: The acting director of the Office of Rent Stabilization went entirely outside his line of duty when he issued a press release explaining why he suspended named subordinates from their positions.

Similarly, a United States Marshal was not absolutely privileged to defame his deputies when publicly explaining his reasons for dismissing them.

A common expression is that an official statement of an officer or employee is absolutely privileged only "if made within the outer perimeter of his line of duty."

ADMINISTRATIVE PROCEEDINGS

Absolute privilege is extended to important administrative proceedings conducted in a manner which affords safeguards customary in a judicial proceeding.

But unless these safeguards are available, an administrative hearing in the lower echelons may not create an occasion of absolute privilege. Statements made at such hearings may be slanderous and actionable, unless made in good faith, without knowledge of the falsity, and for justifiable ends.

> ILLUSTRATION
> Congress directed the Securities and Exchange Commission to make a "study and investigation" of the rules governing national securities exchanges to determine whether the rules adequately protect investors. The SEC set up a study group to do so. During the course of a hearing held in Washington, D.C., witnesses from a leading brokerage firm slandered Engelmohr. He brought suit against the witnesses. The Supreme Court of Washington held that the statements made by the witness at the hearing were not absolutely privileged.

In respect to all occasions of absolute privilege, for publishers the important question is: May we safely repeat what was there said? This is the transition to a qualified privilege.

II. QUALIFIED OR CONDITIONAL PRIVILEGE

Sometimes statements made between two (or among a few) individuals, as between past and prospective employers of an applicant for a job, are conditionally privileged. The rules pertaining to these private communications are here bypassed; publishers and broadcasters are primarily interested in reporting proceedings, occasions, and matters affecting the public generally and in relaying spot news to everybody.

A qualified—a conditional—privilege may arise when it

is more important for the public to be informed about the privileged proceeding or event than it is for an individual to have legal redress. This most frequently occurs in connection with reports of judicial or legislative proceedings and in stories concerning the administration of government. It may also arise regarding publication of matters of more general or public concern although the latitude allowed defamatory utterances in this context is much more circumscribed.

Anyone reporting these and other privileged occasions to the public enjoys a limited privilege. This privilege of telling about these occasions is said to be qualified or conditional because good faith and absence of malice are elements. If qualified privilege is abused, it is forfeited.

The qualifiedly privileged report need not be a verbatim account, but it must be fair and impartial. The qualified privilege applies only to that which happened and was said during the privileged occasion. If the story includes additional facts, the publisher must be prepared to prove the added statements are true.

MAXIMA CONFUSIO IN LIBELLO

The confusion which, in some states, exists in the law of libel has been noted by many writers, both judicial and lay. It is deplored by all. Explorations into the reasons leading to the confusion would end in mere speculation, not worthwhile here.

Significant segments of the law of libel are unique—dissimilar from legal rules with which lawyers and judges are most familiar. Libel cases are relatively few in number. Judges are not ordinarily experienced in the practical application of the esoteric concepts of privilege and fair comment essential to the preservation of freedom of speech and, in turn, of a free society.

And so it is that here and there will be found maverick decisions which distort the law of libel. For instance, for more than a generation an appellate court repeated the whimsical refrain: "Privilege ends where falsity begins." Yet obviously the very essence of the defense of privilege is protection despite falsity. In a five-to-four decision, the majority of a nine-judge appellate court twice said (in essence): "The defense of qualified privilege does not extend to a publication to the entire public." If that were the law, legislative and judicial proceedings could not be reported, except at prohibitive risk, without omitting defamatory remarks, no matter who made them. It is apparent such an error cannot be permitted in a government by and for the people—the "entire public" does have a right to know.

American courts are not alone in finding defamation to be a baffling segment of the law. After a decade of study, a white-wigged committee appointed by the Lord High Chancellor of Great Britain reported the following public consensus:

> The law and practice in actions for defamation are:
> (i) unnecessarily complicated and (ii) unduly costly;
> (iii) such as to make it difficult to forecast the result of an action both as to liability and as to measure of damages;
> (iv) liable to stifle discussion upon matters of public interest and concern (here only we are better off than the British);
> (v) too severe on a defendant who is innocent of any intention to defame; and
> (vi) too favorable to those who, in colloquial language, may be described as "gold-digging" plaintiffs.

It is comparatively easy for society to decide that a negotiable instrument must, among other things, be for a sum certain in money payable to order or bearer. It is exceedingly difficult to determine under what circumstances one citizen should be permitted to malign another. Every jurisdiction is subject to oddities in the law of libel. This is compounded by our unique federal system which sometimes permits different state and national rules—the application of which will be dependent upon the particular facts of the case before the court.

There is no formula that will automatically determine how much reliance may be placed upon each of the myriad variable possible occasions of qualified or conditional privilege. Typical situations must therefore be described, and a practical evaluation made. We now come to that task. In this context the lone word "privilege" often will be used in lieu of the longer expression "conditional or qualified privilege."

CHAPTER 7

PRACTICAL APPLICATION OF QUALIFIED (CONDITIONAL) PRIVILEGES

To abuse it is to lose it.

MACRAE

THE existence of a qualified (a conditional) privilege is founded upon public policy: the recognition that it is essential that a publisher have a right to disseminate information whenever it is necessary to do so for the protection of one's own interest, the interests of third persons, or of the public. The immunity from liability which the privilege offers is extended only when exercised for the purpose for which the privilege was created and with reasonable care that no more injury shall be done to others than is necessary to accomplish a valid end. This caveat becomes critical since the essence of the privilege is publication of defamatory information without liability to the person defamed.

A qualified privilege usually arises when reporting absolutely privileged occasions alluded to in the previous chapter. The defamatory words have already been uttered (published) to those in the courtroom, to the legislators, or to other persons present on an occasion of privilege. So, strictly speaking, media are frequently *re*publishing rather than originating the libel. When referring to media, it is customary to ignore this fine distinction in the use of the words "publish" and *"re*publish." Except in a few instances, we will follow custom.

*Re*publication of defamatory matter in reports of judicial, legislative, executive, or truly public proceedings which deal with matters of public concern is privileged if the report is accurate and complete or a fair abridgment of what has occurred. The privilege is abused—and therefore lost—when the publisher does not give a fair and accurate report of the proceedings.

A less frequent framework for conditional privilege arises where a newspaper prints a letter to the editor, or a radio or television station provides time on the air for a statement which is privileged. This secondary privilege exists in order to make it possible for those who have a privilege in the first instance to find a means of publication, without which their privilege would be of little value. The privilege is conditioned upon the original speaker's actual absolute privilege or (the court should hold) upon the republisher's justifiable belief that the original speaker enjoys an absolute privilege.

When consulting *Say It Safely* in day-to-day operations, the reader may often be under a time pressure. This will be especially so in connection with practical application of the rules of privilege. So we have subdivided this chapter into eleven main subjects (and half a dozen other chapters into fewer subdivisions) to facilitate quick reference in the table of contents to the point you seek. For example: a doubt about a grand jury story would lead you instantly to Part I entitled "Judicial and Pre-Court Proceedings." There you will find the page reference to grand jury. Or the cloudy area of "Public Meetings" will hit you in the eye as Part V.

Of course the index will point to the same pages. But, we think, the breakdown of this long "working" chapter in the table of contents may be of practical value. It will facilitate a quick check-through of other aspects of conditional privilege, one or more of which might be pertinent to your story.

I. Judicial and Pre-Court Proceedings

We now reach the conditions necessary to the utilization of qualified privilege as a defense. First comes practical application to judicial proceedings.

Trials

Everyone may quote false and defamatory matter made in the course of and as part of a trial in open court. Accurate and fair reports of these hearings are guarded by a privilege which is diluted only to the extent that protection is lost if the story is published for the purpose of defaming the individual named rather than to inform the public. This privilege gives protection even though it is known that the defamatory statement is false, unless published with malice.

It is applicable to coverage of proceedings in any court—federal, state, or municipal—whether it is a court of general, or of special and limited, jurisdiction. Except in the most flagrant situations, the reporter need not be concerned with whether the court has lawful jurisdiction of the particular controversy in which it undertakes to act. It is sufficient if the judge assumes jurisdiction.

The judicial proceedings within the rule are not limited to full-dress trials. But neither do they include everything that occurs as an incident to jousts in open court. For instance, statements stricken from the record may not be privileged.

If the person defamed is not a party to the action, an extra check should be made to be sure of identity—is this the individual to whom the judge or witness referred? If an ex parte hearing, this is even more important.

EX PARTE HEARINGS

Sometimes, as on a show-cause order, only one party is before the court. The other has not yet had a chance to be heard. This does not destroy privilege if the matter has come officially before the tribunal and action has been taken.

CAUTION

When only one side has been heard, great care should be used lest the story be unfair to the absent party. The privilege must not be abused. If possible, the explanation of the person defamed should be in the first story. When he has had his day in court, his side of the controversy should be reported with similar prominence.

PLEADING BEFORE JUDICIAL ACTION

A great judge said that in respect to court proceedings a qualified privilege is granted not to satisfy public curiosity about a neighbor's misfortune but to enable the public to watch the court perform its judicial functions and see that justice is evenhanded. Consistent with his theory, in many states the mere filing of a complaint, petition, answer, or similar document with the clerk of the court does not in itself make the contents privileged. In other jurisdictions the privilege attaches at the time the pleadings are filed; the theory in these jurisdictions is that the pleading is a public and official act in the course of a judicial proceeding.

Unless (ask your lawyer) the laws of the states in which your publication circulates or the broadcast is heard are clear to the effect that merely filing such a paper does give rise to a qualified privilege, it should be assumed that there is none.

Assuredly the privilege to repeat contents attaches when a document has been called to the attention of the court and the court has acted. Final disposition of the matter by the court is not required. It is enough if some judicial action has been taken so that in the normal progress of the proceeding a final decision will be rendered.

> Almost always, if a modicum of skill is exercised, a first-class page-one story and headline can be run or a news broadcast safely featured when the complaint or other document is first filed, even before any judicial action is taken. The parties may be named, the nature of the action and the relief sought described, and (except in very rare instances) enough of the allegations recited to round out the story. Usually the omission or toning down of specific defamatory allegations will make the publication secure.

AFFIDAVITS AND SUNDRY COURT PAPERS

What has just been said in respect to pleadings applies generally to affidavits, exhibits, evidentiary instruments, and so on filed with the clerk but not yet presented to the judge.

Practical Application of Qualified Privileges

Sometimes a zealous reporter (we hope discreetly) prearranges with counsel to the end that the newsworthy item is brought to the attention of the court for action—of course at a propitious hour in relation to deadlines. Then the story is privileged, though perhaps subject to attack for abuse of privilege.

A *possible situation:* The reporter and the lawyer who seeks publicity for his case connive for privilege for a sensational story. The suit fails and, in due course, the opposing party commences a counter-offense based on malicious prosecution. Has the publisher conspired with the reckless lawyer to publicize a malicious and unfounded proceeding and thus become a conspirator?

DEPOSITIONS

Ordinarily, depositions of parties or witnesses are not privileged until read in court or the contents otherwise brought to the attention of the judge for action. Beware of depositions released by publicity-conscious lawyers prior to consideration by the court.

CORONER'S JURY

The actual verdict of a coroner's jury is privileged unless it is apparent the procedure was irregular, the verdict was not reached in good faith, or it contains defamatory matter not pertinent to the inquiry. Sometimes the inquiry before a coroner's jury is one-sided with no chance for an accused to be heard. Sometimes the accused is present and is afforded an opportunity to testify and examine witnesses. Accordingly, when an inquest is reported, discrimination must be used.

SAY IT SAFELY

CAUTION

If, for instance, a verdict reads, "Death by poisoning," but does not name the person who administered the vial, disproportionate risk is assumed if the suspected person is named, unless the story gives a fair and impartial account of his testimony.

GRAND JURIES

A grand jury conducts a secret inquisition. There is no carte blanche to repeat everything said before or reported by a grand jury, even after its indictment or report has been presented to the court.

Some grand juries have statutory power to investigate public institutions and other public affairs and to make reports concerning them. Other grand juries—including federal—have only the right to indict or ignore; such a jury has no right to make a report of any kind. Its "report" might have no privilege at all, except as a matter of great public importance and concern. When publishing the report of a grand jury, know whether the latitude is present which follows a report directed or authorized by statute. When excerpts are published, be sure it is done fairly, without libelous implications running beyond the privileged report.

The news story may say the grand jury was critical of, or severely condemned, the subject of its inquiry, but should not recite libelous details unless clearly in the public interest or included in an indictment.

CAUTION

Grand jury reports containing libelous imputations upon private citizens or upon public officers not touching their fitness for office or their fidelity to the public service or the propriety of official acts must be handled circumspectly.

Indictments may be described and those indicted named. The story may of course be rounded out to the extent proper whenever a criminal charge is filed against a person presumably innocent.

INDICTMENTS, INFORMATIONS, WARRANTS FOR ARREST

There is a qualified privilege when publishing the charge contained in an information, indictment, or warrant for arrest. Here privilege combines with the easily provable truth that the charge was actually filed, so long (but only so long) as the story stays by the court record. Often the off-the-record statements of law enforcement officers contain real news, but, as will be seen, except in rare instances these carry little or no privilege.

CAUTIONS

1. It should be remembered that a suspect is presumed innocent until proved guilty. It may be proper to say, "Jones was arrested and questioned" but libelous to say, "Burglar is caught" or "Hunted criminal is found." When no indictment, information, or warrant has been issued, the story should usually be limited to a statement such as, "Blank was arrested and is being held" in connection with the case.

2. Expressions such as "suspect grilled" should not be used until a charge has been filed. The suspect may be exonerated, never charged with crime, and then may sue, claiming that he was being questioned only as a possible witness.

3. If it is manifest that the charging officer has gone beyond the customary language of a charge and, for instance, unnecessarily maligned third persons, the material should be handled charily.

Reports of preliminary proceedings before a magistrate as well as of the trial itself are privileged.

POLICE NEWS

Strictly speaking, police news emanates from an administrative arm of government. Because it usually attends or precedes a judicial proceeding, we treat it here.

The suspicions and theories, the clues and forecasts, and the reports of law enforcement officers seeking publicity often accompany criminal charges. These statements are not privileged. Privilege must be based on one or more of the several occasions already discussed.

> CAUTION
> The report by an officer that the prisoner has confessed is not privileged. It may be true, but sometimes a prisoner denies that he confessed. The publisher must be prepared to prove the confession was made. Confessions that implicate others have added hazards.
> Sometimes confessions are lost by the police. In dubious cases it is prudent to photograph the confession so that it will be available when needed.

Much study has been given by bench, bar, and the Fourth Estate to the handling of news of crimes. Chapter 16 is devoted to freedom of speech vis-à-vis fair trials.

II. LEGISLATIVE PROCEEDINGS

The conditional privilege applicable to judicial proceedings in open court extends its protection to fair reports of legislative debate and action.

ON THE FLOOR

If the distinguished senator from Utah forgets senatorial courtesy and when the Senate is in session says defamatory things about the distinguished senator from New York, the people have a right to know of the fracas. A fair account may be published locally or broadcast to every hamlet in the Empire State without fear of actionable libel. The protection is the same, regardless of whom the senator attacks from the floor of the Senate, or a representative defames from the floor of the House.

The privilege protects a story when it tells of the official proceedings of any state legislature. It applies also, but not necessarily with full force, to the official proceedings of a city or town council, school board, county commissioners, or other official municipal body. But discretion must be used when repeating irrelevant libels uttered before minor legislative groups.

CAUTION
Recall the periodic challenge of one legislator to another to "say that off the floor so I can sue you for libel"? The privilege attaches to official proceedings, not to personal vendettas outside the legislative hall.

Impeachment proceedings are within the privilege.

COMMITTEE HEARINGS

Committees are part of the legislative process. Some hearings are conducted with pomp and paraphernalia comparable to an important court proceeding. Some are informal. Some are secret.

Certainly a vigorous qualified privilege attaches to reports of a formal legislative hearing, open to the public. In contrast, discretion must be used when reciting what the reporter believes happened (citing impeccable but unnamed sources) at a hearing where the public was barred. The official report of the committee is privileged; a leak as to what the report will say is not. If defamatory, it is dangerous. The report itself may be different.

What has just been said applies to the committees of the Congress, state legislatures, and important municipal legislative bodies—including port commissions, school boards, sewer or water or flood commissions, and so on. As the status descends from the Congress to the municipal level, increasing care must be taken to make sure that the hearing meets the basic tests necessary to a foundation for qualified privilege.

It should not be assumed that the full qualified privilege applies to stories of the excesses of every petty local committee, particularly when not germane to the public questions before it.

> ILLUSTRATION TO THE CONTRARY
> During (or possibly at a special conference after) a session of the city council, in response to questioning by a councilman, the city manager said he was not going to promote two police officers because they were insubordinate and should have been fired. The Passaic *Daily News* had a qualified privilege to publish the report.

The defamatory remarks pertained strictly to the conduct of the policemen while on duty—did not accuse either of a crime or attack them personally.

III. EXECUTIVE PROCEEDINGS

We are now examining the qualified privilege which protects repetition of libelous statements made in the course of executive—administrative—proceedings.

TOP LEVEL PROCEEDINGS

Fair reports of formal executive hearings of high order carry a privilege equivalent to that for reports of judicial or legislative proceedings. It is assumed that the hearings on this plateau:

 (i) are pursuant to statutory authority or inaugurated by an official of highest rank (usually the president, a cabinet officer or a governor, or the head of an important branch of government);

 (ii) are carried out by federal, state, or, *with considerable caution*, county, municipal, and special governmental agencies such as school districts or port commissions;

(iii) will be conducted with a certain formality and will appear to be keeping within an authorized sphere;

 (iv) are open to the public;

and that:

 (v) protection somewhat analogous to that of a court proceeding is afforded to the persons who are the subjects of the investigation and to witnesses;

 (vi) third parties who are defamed will be given an opportunity to clear their names if they so desire.

If these conditions are met, executive proceedings may be reported.

The problem arises so often that it may be worthwhile to restate the guidelines: When reporting the proceedings of an administrative committee, do not assume it to be an occasion of absolute privilege which assures the publisher of a secure occasion of qualified privilege if he accurately reports what was there said, *unless* the committee is clearly an orderly group, proceeding (i) under statutory authority, or (ii) at the direction of the president, a governor, cabinet officer, or other high executive acting within his sphere, or (iii) is constituted by an administrative board or body while performing functions authorized by law.

Secondary Hearings and Investigations; Administrative Proceedings

As executive proceedings decline in dignity and public importance, it is necessary to be more alert than in the case of judicial proceedings in an established court. A court is a court, even though the judicial officer be a rural justice of the peace, unlearned in the law, perhaps not even authorized to practice law. Executive proceedings may grade down from a Warren Commission studying the assassination of a president to quizzing by a petty official—perhaps with no statutory authorization to conduct the inquisition.

So executive hearings (administrative proceedings) must be considered on their merits. An inquiry by the mayor of a village does not enjoy the status equal to that of an extradition proceeding or a hearing incident to a proposed pardon or an investigation into important affairs of the commonwealth by or on behalf of a governor.

IV. Quoting Public Statements by Officials

Public statements *by* important governmental officials are the subject of this section. Stories *about* public officials are covered in Part VI of this chapter, and editorials which castigate them in Chapter 8.

General Rules

Statements by public officials fall into three classes:

(i) those made in course of official duties and strictly limited to things germane to a problem within the jurisdiction of the official; *or*

(ii) in part devoted to matters of public concern and in

part to defamatory digressions not important to the presentation of the public matters being discussed; *or*

(iii) with little or no ground for asserting that any of the statements are in the public weal.

A qualified privilege attends repetition of statements within class (i). Obviously libelous statements which are in class (iii) should not be repeated unless the publisher is prepared to prove substantial truth.

If the statement falls in class (ii), consummate care must be used before repeating a libel per se—was it a necessary or at least a proper part of the handling of a matter of public consequence within the orbit of this official or reporting to the public in respect thereto? Or was it part of the ramblings of a politician?

ILLUSTRATIONS:

1. The governor of Arkansas held a press conference and released a "Press Statement of Governor Faubus." The release dealt with irregularities in nursing homes and improper acts by nursing home proprietors. He characterized conditions as a "sordid and shocking story of mismanagement and misdeeds."

The *Gazette* sent a reporter to one of the homes to interview management. It published the governor's statement plus a denial of the charges by the home. The newspaper won the libel suit because of: (i) qualified privilege, the good faith demonstrated by the careful reporting and publication of the denials by the accused, and (ii) consent to publication given incident to the reporter's visit to the home and interview with plaintiff.

Note that plaintiff sued despite fair treatment and apparent consent.

2. The Scranton *Times* published an abridged report of an investigation made at the direction of Governor Averill

Harriman of New York into the activities and associations of those known to have been at a meeting of underworld overlords and their vassals. The plaintiff was a delegate. The report mentioned an arrest on rape charges and association with racketeers in his biographical sketch.

The Supreme Court of Pennsylvania decided: (i) the governor of New York enjoyed absolute immunity when publishing the report; (ii) because it is in the public interest that information be made available as to what takes place in public affairs, the newspaper had a qualified privilege when it told of the report; (iii) the article as a whole was a fair and substantially correct summary of the governmental report; the qualified privilege had not been abused.

The points relied upon by the Pennsylvania court constitute a typical—a classic—design of the three cornerstones to privilege.

3. A director of the Internal Revenue Service issued a press release stating that assets of plaintiff had been seized to satisfy delinquent income taxes. The *News-Journal* ran a story. The director misspoke. *Held:* The district director had either an absolute or qualified privilege as to the press release. Therefore, the newspaper had a qualified privilege when repeating it in good faith without knowledge of the falsity.

The district director was considered to be a policy-making official of the executive branch of government. His area of discretion included the drastic action he erroneously said was taken against a citizen.

Police, prosecuting attorneys, and other law enforcement officials have wide powers—a man may be charged with murder. Yet, as has been seen, more often than not their public statements are devoid of privilege. Except when quoting a summit official, sound judgment must be used.

Under one set of circumstances it would be safe—it might be a duty to the public—to quote an announcement by the chairman of the Port Commission. On another occasion the answer might be "no qualified privilege." Absent duty to the public, when secondary officials are the speakers, play safe. The essentials can be told sans libel.

RARE EXCEPTIONS

There is an occasional exception. It is libelous to say a columnist or newscaster is a liar. The president of the United States calls one a liar on an occasion of no privilege under ordinary rules. Because of the eminence of the speaker, what he said may be repeated. But not so, if a congressman said the same when not on the floor of the House, unless it is possible to tie to another type of privilege.

The illustration just given does not warrant an inference that privileged statements stem only from top officials. But as the rank becomes lower, those who repeat the official defamation must use increasing care to make sure it is made incident to official duties and is directly related to the performance of official functions.

QUOTING OFFICEHOLDERS AS CANDIDATES

When the public official who might be safely quoted as a public official performing the functions of his office becomes a candidate for re-election, other principles apply. The strict legal rule is that there is no qualified privilege when:

(i) perpetuating the defamations of a vicious or careless candidate by print or broadcast; or

(ii) publishing or repeating his ads or other written material.

Such should be assumed to be the law, except in important situations where the officeholder seeks to oust another—a legislator runs for governor—a greater latitude might be allowed in view of the *New York Times* decision elsewhere discussed.

When checking the accuracy of news stories a reporter may be held to a higher standard of performance than is expected of a candidate for elective office when—in the heat of the campaign—he assembles materials for campaign propaganda.

Spot News

Situations can occur when spot news—in contrast to ads—may, almost must, be published even though libelous, because of the importance of the candidate and the occasion of the utterance. At the apex would be a president or a governor seeking re-election. His libel is an ad-lib uttered during a television interview. Millions hear it. As a practical matter, he will be quoted by most news media. Similar considerations apply to spot news reporting a vicious attack on a high official by the rival candidate.

Grading down to tertiary offices where a libel should not be repeated, no matter how newsworthy, a rule of reason may be applied by management in telling what officeholders as candidates have actually said on important occasions. These comments do not apply to what their followers say unless the speaker is of great eminence and the news story almost inescapable.

There are lowly considerations which may have a bearing

when weighing the risk. To illustrate: It may be safer to publish the story of a libel about the winning candidate than the man destined to defeat. If the defamed candidate is elected, it is most unlikely he will sue a publisher who has given him fair coverage. Certainly not if the publisher has happened to support him editorially and has given him favorable publicity. He will want continued support.

But what if the candidate is defeated by a narrow margin and the libel per se was circulated or broadcast shortly before election day? Truth may be the only defense. The judge should instruct the jury that no special damages may be allowed for the defeat on election day. That pleasant sounding instruction may prove to be of little or no aid to the defendant. There being a libel per se, the jury may bring in a verdict sufficient to buy a press or rebuild the tower, unless truth has been proved.

The statutory responsibilities of radio and television in respect to political broadcasts are delineated in Chapter 14.

V. Public Meetings

Some recent authorities take the position that a conditional privilege extends to reports of any gathering which is open to the general public and is held for the purpose of discussing matters of public concern. By supplying them with information about public events, the publisher is acting as the "eyes and ears" of people who do not attend.

The privilege applies even though admission to the meeting is charged so long as anyone is free to pay it. (We noticed no case hinging on the point of excessive price.)

The privilege does not apply to reports of private meetings or to reports of public meetings which do not deal with matters of public concern.

ILLUSTRATIONS:

1. In the midst of a vitriolic, aggressive campaign candidates staged a public meeting at which they and their supporters spoke. In the course of the spectacle, Jones, a candidate for office, made defamatory statements of fact concerning his opponent, Smith. The newspaper ran a complete and accurate report of the meeting, including the defamatory statements. The newspaper report should be held to be conditionally privileged.

2. A corporation held its annual meeting of shareholders; it was not open to the public. In the course of the meeting, Blather, one of the shareholders, made false and defamatory statements concerning the president and treasurer of the company. A complete and accurate report of the meeting including the defamatory statements appeared in the local newspapers and was broadcast on both radio and television. The stories were not privileged.

3. Plaintiff, a prominent real estate developer, was attempting to persuade the city council to grant a zoning variance on certain land which he owned. The city desired to purchase another parcel of land owned by him for a public purpose. In the course of negotiations about the purchase price, plaintiff indicated that agreeing to the city's offer might depend upon his being granted the zoning variance. At the council meeting a member of the council described this position as "blackmail." The defendant, Greenbelt, a newspaper publisher, published a full and accurate account of the council meeting including a description of plaintiff's negotiating tactics. It quoted the "blackmail" statement made by the city councilman. The court denied plaintiff's claim against Greenbelt. The newspaper was performing its proper function when it reported the debates. The article was privileged.

VI. Defamation of Public Officials

Rules that govern the people's right to know what goes on in public affairs have been changing rapidly.

Departing from the traditional strict rule requiring proof

of truth, courts began to recognize it is no longer realistic to assume that even the largest publisher or broadcaster has personnel sufficient to investigate every facet of public affairs and to prove that every statement touching the administration of government is true. Publication deadlines and the need to print today's news make it extremely difficult to conduct a thorough investigation in every instance.

In response to the public's need to know what is happening in government, and now pursuant to the First and Fourteenth Amendments to the Constitution (Chapter 19), a general rule began to evolve to the effect that if the publisher in good faith believes the statement to be true, has made a fair investigation or has received his news in the belief that a fair investigation has been made, and publishes or broadcasts in good faith, without malice, plaintiff may not recover damages for defamatory matter in the publication. As stated by the Supreme Court of West Virginia:

> . . . a citizen of a free state having an interest in the conduct of the affairs of his government should not be held to strict accountability for a misstatement of fact, if he has tried to ascertain the truth and, on a reasonable basis, honestly and in good faith believes that the statements made by him are true.

Dismissing a libel suit brought by a congressman based upon a newspaper article charging him with anti-Semitism, an eminent federal judge said:

> Cases which impose liability for erroneous reports of the political conduct of officials reflect the obsolete doctrine that the governed must not criticize their governors. . . . The protection of the public requires not merely discussion, but information. . . . Errors of fact, particularly in regard to a man's mental state and processes, are inevitable.

Such was the direction of the law. But it could not be said to be the law generally until the *New York Times* decision by the United States Supreme Court.

The *Times* published an ad which described the maltreatment of Negro students protesting segregation, bombings, and other disgraceful conduct in Montgomery, Alabama. Certain of the factual statements were clearly libelous per se. Some were false statements. Were they privileged?

The court made its decision against the background of a profound national commitment to the principle that debate on public issues should be uninhibited and robust and that it may well include vehement, caustic, and sometimes unpleasantly sharp attacks on government and public officials.

The ad was an expression of grievance and protest on a major public issue. The question was whether the falsities forfeited the freedom of expression upon public questions secured by the Constitution.

Recognizing that erroneous statement is inevitable in free debate, the court held that the constitutional guaranty of freedom of speech and press affords a publisher latitude regarding honest mistake when discussing public officials. Public persons are, as it were, public property.

Before the official may recover damages for a defamatory falsehood *relating to his official conduct* or his fitness or role in his official position he must prove the statement was made with actual malice—that is, with knowledge that it was false or with reckless disregard of whether or not it was false.

Public officials have been held to include at least those governmental employees who have, or appear to the public to have, substantial responsibility for or control over the conduct of governmental affairs. The position must be one which would invite public scrutiny and discussion occasioned by the particular charges in controversy.

The extent to which a statement reaching the purely *private* conduct of a public official should be treated as affecting him in his *public* capacity cannot be reduced to a specific rule. The prudent publisher will always exercise caution when dealing in this area.

VII. DEFAMATION OF PUBLIC FIGURES

The Supreme Court has held the constitutional protection also applies to the discussion of "public figures." No precise definition of the term "public figure" has been given. A case by case evolution provides the following guidelines as to two types of public figures.

> 1. Persons who achieve such pervasive fame or notoriety that they become public figures for most purposes;
> 2. Persons who voluntarily inject themselves or are drawn into a particular public controversy and thereby become public figures for a limited range of issues.

The mere carrying of news stories does not turn an event into a public controversy or a plaintiff into a public figure. There must be something of public importance on which to build.

A well known college football coach accused of bribery and a retired army general who had taken prominent controversial positions regarding racial segregation were each found by the Supreme Court to be public figures. Other persons held to come within the rule included non-incumbent candidates for public office, a captain in a sheriff's office, the chairman of a political party, a judicial candidate, a labor leader, and a Nobel prize winner. By engaging in public discussion of controversial matters, these individuals all became "public figures" and their ability to recover damages in a defamation action was limited by the *Times* rule even though the publication about them was defamatory and contained falsities.

VIII. DEFAMATION OF PRIVATE PERSONS OR OF PUBLIC PERSONS IN RELATION TO PRIVATE AFFAIRS

Significant shifts in the law have occurred incident to actions for defamation brought by private persons, that is, individuals who are not public officials or public figures.

Until recently it appeared as if the law might change its focus from the character of the plaintiff to the nature of the controversy. In a case involving the defamation of a distributor of nudist magazines, a plurality of the Supreme Court appeared to extend the *Times* rule to events of public or general concern. For a while "public interest" seemed to be the criterion for applying the *Times* rule. The public's constitutional right to engage in free speech was limited only by the subject matter of debate and not by the characterization of the person defamed.

Other courts in interpreting this decision applied the *Times* limitation to almost any newsworthy event.

This trend was aborted by a majority of the Supreme Court in the *Gertz* case. There a publication was sued by an attorney named Gertz who was falsely charged with framing a policeman for murder. The article falsely called him a communist. Gertz was a private citizen but he was involved in a matter of public interest (the murder trial of a policeman).

Instead of extending the *Times* rule to these facts, the court limited it to matters concerning public officials or public figures. As to private individuals, the Court announced the individual states were free to formulate a legal remedy for defamatory falsehood injurious to the reputation of private individuals "so long as they do not impose liability without fault."

In response to this holding, the American Law Institute has drafted what it believes *should be* the applicable rule. Its pronouncement states:

> One who publishes a false and defamatory communication concerning a private person, or concerning a public official or a public figure in relation to a purely private matter, a private matter not affecting his conduct, fitness, or role in his public capacity, is subject to liability, if, but only if, he
> (a) knows that the statement is false and that it defames the other,
> (b) acts in reckless disregard of these matters, or
> (c) acts negligently in failing to ascertain them.

Sections (a), (b), and (c) comprise the elements of "fault" which must exist before liability can be found. No prudent publisher will knowingly publish a defamatory falsehood. Put another way: The question may be whether the publisher knew or, in the exercise of reasonable care, should have known the statement was false or would create a false impression in some material respect. Was he negligent?

Media and media personnel will be held to the skill and experience normally possessed by professionally proficient members of the Fourth Estate. Custom in the area, though not controlling, will be relevant in applying the negligence standard.

While the standard of care itself will not change, its application may vary with the circumstances. For example, time deadlines may preclude an absolutely thorough investigation, especially when the medium is dealing with hot news. And a jury may decide that desire to make a deadline is no excuse for an inadequate investigation and resulting defamation. The court will consider these factors when deciding the issues in a defamation suit; judicial viewpoints will vary. Trial judges may have been reared in the tradition that "he who publishes a libel per se does so at his peril." The arguments of defense counsel to the point that such a rule may no longer be constitutional may:

(i) not impress the judge, or
(ii) result in the judge formally bowing to the constitutional inhibition but giving an instruction on negligence which will make it very easy for the jury to decide for the plaintiff.

And so it is that publishers must remember that they may be haled before a trial judge who will wish to hold a publisher liable for defamation (particularly a libel per se) upon slight showing of fault. Liability, of course, will be subject to the defense of substantial truth and to the defenses of privilege and fair comment.

Good journalism dictates that the accuracy of all news be verified as thoroughly as possible. The more time before publication deadline the greater the opportunity for investigation and verification. In all cases, however, the publisher will make sure the potential target of a defamatory statement is interviewed (or a real attempt is made to interview him) for his side of the story. *His version should be given as prominent coverage as the charges.* If the subject refuses to comment, or cannot be reached for comment, that should be put into the story. A jury will want to know what you did to investigate the truth of the matter before publishing. If this question is answered within the story, the jury will be reminded of your careful preparation each time it reads or views it. Moreover, it removes the devastating argument which plaintiff's counsel will invariably make to the effect that "they published this story without even trying to verify it with my client."

It should be emphasized that the *Gertz* case does not say that states may not apply the *Times* rule to publications about matters of public controversy. They may, and several have. Thus, whether in such matters the *Times* standard or a negligence or other standard applies will vary from state to state. Your lawyers can advise you as to the current law in your publication or broadcast area.

As has been observed when reckoning the strength of a qualified privilege, the importance of the event must be considered. The conduct of a colonel would usually give rise to no more than a faint privilege. If he were in command of troops brought in to quell plundering after a flood, his activities might be subject to detailed scrutiny, and if libel were to slip in there would be a qualified privilege. But neighborhood interest is not enough. There must be a widespread public interest in a matter of consequence to government or the welfare of the people, and the challenged statement must be related to the public welfare.

Material libelous per se should not be published in *sole* reliance upon the importance of the event without deliberate assumption of the risk by management. Occasionally there may be another privilege to which to tie.

IX. Sundry Situations

Recall and Other Petitions

Assertions of a recall petition not directed to efficiency or competency in office but to the officeholder's private life or honesty carry no privilege. If the story adheres to the language of a bona fide petition directed to conduct in public office, it is qualifiedly privileged.

But if the story goes beyond the petition, the publisher may be put to prove the truth of the libel. There should be no implication of guilt beyond the precise language of the petition.

These comments apply to other official petitions—recognized by statute—in respect to public affairs.

REPLIES TO ATTACKS

One who has been attacked by another has the right of self-defense. The role of publishers in such a situation is discussed in Chapter 9. When there is a broadcast by a political candidate, this right is clearly set forth under FCC regulations, as will be noted in Chapter 14.

SEMIPUBLIC PROCEEDINGS

In contrast to truly public proceedings, there is no privilege when reporting private gatherings—church, society, lodge, stockholders' meetings, conventions, and the like—unless, because of unusual circumstances, the matter is of paramount public importance. Political meetings afford no privilege, except in particular cases when the public interest justifies it.

There are exceptions. For example, an ecclesiastical trial may occur before a tribunal duly constituted by church law. If the proceeding is open to the public and is a matter of public importance, there may be a qualified privilege. But all factors should be weighed.

When the legislature has given a medical or bar association or other semipublic body authority in respect to admission and discipline, its public proceedings may carry a certain privilege.

LABOR DISPUTES

Labor disputes range from private dueling with no qualified privilege when publishing the recriminations of the warring factions, to major battles affecting everyone. The halting of transportation, a shut-down of essential utilities, the closing of hospitals, and many other casualties cannot be minimized nor can they be described without quotations from spokesmen for each side. Sometimes there is a clear privilege when quoting an official speaking in line of duty. More often it is a question of sound practical judgment in the framework of public interest and necessity.

ILLUSTRATION
A newspaper published a letter from a union to employers. It announced the commencement of picketing. The article commented that: (i) the letter threatened "blackmail picketing," (ii) the picketing would be used as a "gangster gun," and (iii) the union did not care for the desires or rights of employees. The Supreme Court of Kansas held that *under the circumstances* there was no libel per se.

"Under the circumstances" means criteria to be considered by management when forecasting whether publication will be privileged.

INNOCENT THIRD PARTIES

Caveats have already been given in respect to thoughtlessly naming innocent third parties. As the quality of the occasion of qualified privilege declines from the strong-

MILLS COLLEGE
LIBRARY

est occasions—typically, legislative proceedings—to the weaker—for example, a village committee hearing—it becomes even more important to guard against libeling innocent third parties not in any way participants in those less significant proceedings.

Ticker, teletype, or other private wire services as well as typesetters and stenographers who transcribe and mail (publish) letters are protected by a qualified privilege.

X. Loss of Privilege; Weighing the Risk

Two dozen occasions of qualified privilege have been described. They range from solid privilege (e.g., reporting a trial) to frail occasions, such as a press release by a county commissioner. One must be either clumsy or negligent to lose the former. The preservation of the latter is to the credit of an informed and alert staff.

The rule of the *Times* case is not a license for thoughtless handling of articles concerning officials, candidates, and others on a public forum. The challenged libel must (i) relate to his conduct, fitness, or role in official position, and (ii) be made without actual malice. If there is knowledge of the falsity or a reckless disregard of truth or falsity, a court or jury may find actual malice. These are factual questions; they may be submitted to an antagonistic jury.

Certainly if the reporter, rewrite man, broadcaster, or editor on duty knew of the falsity, that knowledge would be imputed to the publisher. What if one of them should have been alerted to possible falsity by facts or even rumors within his knowledge, yet he did not double check? Perhaps the records in the publisher's library prove falsity, yet they were not examined. A jury may find this a reckless disregard of truth. Illustrations abound.

There is the constant hazard that antagonists may attack each other in respect to matters not germane to public office or affairs. Such libels are not within the privilege. It is a fair forecast that within the next decade damages will be amerced against publishers whose personnel have over-reached in reliance on the *Times* decision.

IDENTIFYING THE OCCASION OR PERSON

In Chapter 5 it was remarked that when a source is quoted it should be identified. Whenever privilege is present, the nature of that privilege should be revealed in the publication or broadcast so that all will know the origin of the assertions.

ILLUSTRATION
Secret Service men were quoted as charging Hughes and wife with making and passing bogus money. The article itself neither mentioned the Secretary of the Treasury nor intimated that it was reporting an official statement by him. When sued, the newspaper attributed the announcement to the Secretary of the Treasury.
The court held that undisclosed similarity or coincidence between a defendant's libelous statement and a public official's previous announcement is not enough to make the statement a report of the official announcement.

In the above illustration the court did not decide whether qualified privilege would extend to the report of such an "announcement" by the Secretary of the Treasury. If he speaks within the outer periphery of his official functions, he may be safely quoted. Suppose a deputy rather than a cabinet officer made the announcement. Whether he should charge named persons (presumably innocent) with passing bad checks is questionable. That is within the jurisdiction of law enforcement officers. It must always be remembered that the accused may be found "not guilty." The safer course would be to withhold names until a specific charge is in the records of the court.

ABUSE OF PRIVILEGE

If a conditional privilege is misused, it may be destroyed and lost as a defense. Privileges are not self-executing.

The fact that the story tells of a privileged occasion is not in itself enough. It must be consistent with the purposes of the qualified privilege. It must be an impartial (historical) account of the privileged event which included the defamation. The story may be lively, even sensational, but it must not distort. It must not be inaccurate, inflammatory, vicious, or malicious when reciting the defamatory statements made in the course of a privileged event.

In respect to accuracy, media are not held to the scientific precision demanded in, for example, technical reporting. It is enough if the article gives a substantially correct account of what happened. But a publisher may lose his privilege and subject himself to liability by publishing for the purpose of harming the person defamed, by publication to persons to whom the privilege does not extend, by repetition after the privilege has passed, or by inclusion of unprivileged defamatory matter.

The *Village Voice* was recently reminded that the *Times* v. *Sullivan* doctrine may not be stretched too far. It ran an ad in the *New York Times* rather than in its own publication. The ad quoted previous Voice articles highly critical of a local judge. So, like the Sullivan case, it involved a public official and a matter of public interest. The New York Court held that this "house ad" for *Village Voice* was not entitled to protection under *Times* v. *Sullivan*. The United States Supreme Court declined to review the New York decision. Perhaps the important caveat in this case is that if you publish libel in an advertisement promoting yourself you do so at your peril.

WHEN PRIVILEGE IS NOT CLEAR

As already emphasized, when the occasion is not clearly one that affords a reliable privilege, the publisher's position is strengthened by including statements from the person defamed. These should be given a prominence similar to the charges against him. Even the sentence "John Doe could not be reached for comment" helps somewhat. It shows a desire to give an impartial account.

WEIGHING THE RISK

Words and circumstances are infinite in number and character. Permissible stories cannot be catalogued. Often the degree (amount) of protection actually afforded by an occasion of qualified privilege cannot be estimated without precise knowledge of the occasion which is believed to create the privilege to repeat.

Editorial and managerial discretion must be used, taking into consideration:

  (i) the importance to the public of the subject under discussion;
 (ii) the eminence of the public officer or the nature of the public proceeding;
(iii) the circumstances of the utterance;
 (iv) the *provable* reputation of the person defamed;
  (v) whether because of other relevant and provable of-

fenses he is in any position to bring suit against the publisher; and

(vi) all other facts and circumstances.

The expression "other relevant and provable offenses" needs illustration. Here is an actual sequence, typical of a situation when it can be proved that the accused did do something else just as bad which is sufficiently related to the story in question:

A reputable husband was suspected of murdering his second wife. The first stories were written warily. Suddenly the body was found, and he made an easily provable confession. The field became wide open—headlines announced, "Husband Confesses Murder." Then he was suspected of having murdered his first wife. This he hotly denied. His denials mentioned third persons, connecting them with the disappearance of his first wife. As to the husband, the easily provable confession in respect to wife number two made safe enough the publication or broadcast of the details of the investigation of the death of wife number one.* But prudence indicated utmost caution concerning the third persons mentioned by Bluebeard.

XI. A REVIEW

Affairs public proliferate. More and more events occur in the twilight zones of privilege. A partial review may be useful.

The cautious course is to assume that only those statements of a public official or public figure that are clearly within the orbit of his duties may be repeated with confidence. Only then is the repetition secure behind the barrier of conditional privilege. A presidential press confer-

---

* Whether such details should be published is a subject considered in Chapter 16, "Free Speech—Fair Trial."

ence is not an official proceeding. Yet surely any statement on public affairs thus openly made by the president of the United States can be safely passed along.

Unofficial statements by lesser personages grade down to zero so far as privilege to repeat is concerned. In a matter of great public importance, the statement of the mayor of New York, speaking as mayor and not as a politician, might be repeated with confidence that, as a practical matter, there is a certain protection—a sort of extralegal practical privilege—if true conditional privilege fails. The utterances of a small town mayor or chairman of an irrigation district might have no such additional extralegal sanctity.

Similarly, there is, by legal rule, a most vigorous conditional privilege in telling of legislative proceedings. But in practice the courts and juries may not grant the same protection when reporting the antics of a meeting of county commissioners as when reporting the deliberations of the Senate of the United States. As to the former, a court or jury may more quickly find an abuse of privilege, whatever the legal theories may be.

The practical result is that statements made before a city council, for instance, cannot always be repeated with the same confidence in a shield of privilege as statements made on the floor of the Congress or a state legislature.

In Part I, Chapter 6, under the heading "Administrative Proceedings," note was made of an SEC hearing which lacked certain attributes of a proceeding which carries an absolute privilege. A witness at that hearing was held liable for his slanders. Would the repetition of the testimony (via broadcast or print, making it a libel) be protected by a qualified privilege? Probably not, unless the overriding public importance of the subject or the witness makes the news account a public duty—to be performed with utmost caution.

95

SAY IT SAFELY

Whenever an occasion is deficient in factors assuring absolute privilege, libelous statements not strictly germane to the public question involved should be eschewed, and even if relevant, should be repeated cautiously making sure that the person defamed has an opportunity to give his version of the story.

CHAPTER 8

COMMENT AND CRITICISM

It is much easier to be critical than to be correct.

DISRAELI

THE defense of qualified privilege applies to defamatory statements of fact. The common law defense of fair comment (sometimes called privileged criticism) applies to defamatory comments. The one permits factual statements; the other permits expressions of opinion which otherwise would cause actionable damage.

Fact and comment do not dwell in sharply divided compartments. They mingle in the same speech or editorial— frequently in the same paragraph. Not unnaturally, court decisions sometimes treat the two as almost alike. Nevertheless, there are important distinctions between qualified privilege and fair comment. The essence may be stated thus:

A false assertion of fact would be an actionable libel unless there were a privilege to say or repeat the libelous statement.

Fair comment is an opinion fairly stated in relation to provable facts and (with caution) recitals clearly privileged. It is no libel.

In short: One is a libel against which there is a defense; the other is not a libel.

I. WHO MAY BE CRITICIZED

Natural subjects of criticism and adverse comment include public officials (judges, legislators, and executives); candidates for public office; public institutions; matters of public concern (including the work of independent contractors being paid out of public funds); scientific, artistic, literary works; dramatic productions and exhibitions; and sporting events catering to the public.

Groups dedicated, in whole or in part, to influencing public opinion or changing the laws or customs of the land—from a manufacturers' association to a labor union and from the Ku Klux Klan to CORE—are subject to comment and criticism.

An organization which publicly solicits funds for the support of its activities should expect the white light of inquiry and comment. The same may be said of an individual who enters the public arena, though not a candidate.

It has been emphasized that the degree—the quality—of qualified privilege varies with the occasion—for instance, a United States senator vis-à-vis a deputy sheriff.

In similar fashion the freedom to criticize varies with the subject of the criticism. The shield is strongest when criticizing public officials. So officeholders will be first considered, and then candidates. The discussions in Chapter 7 apply in part to comment as well as to news reports.

PUBLIC OFFICIALS—THE STRICT RULE

The traditional rule (once sound, but by changed conditions rendered harsh and now outmoded by the *Times* decision) is that the comment is fair when:

1. It is based on facts *provably* true.
2. It is free of imputations of corrupt or dishonorable motives on the part of the person who is criticized except insofar as such imputations are warranted by the facts.
3. It is an honest expression of opinion—the motive is the public weal, not desire to harm.

THE MARCH TOWARD REALITY

Responsive to these changed conditions (even before the *Times* and Gertz decisions and based on the factors just indicated rather than the federal Constitution), a more liberal rule has been supplanting the old. Under this more realistic approach, a misstatement of fact about a public official or public figure in connection with matters of public concern, is privileged. Hence, there is a defense to the libel action if the statement is made for the benefit of the public, in the absence of malice, and in the honest belief that it is true. As indicated, "honest belief" presupposes care in gathering the news or receipt from a reliable source.

PUBLIC OFFICIALS—THE RIGHT RULE

The ad before the court in the *New York Times* case was mixed fact and criticism. Privilege for the citizen—critic of officialdom—was sanctified. "It is as much his duty to criticize as it is the official's duty to administer." The rule now is that, since the Constitution requires recognition of the conditional privilege for honest misstatement of fact, it follows that a defense of fair comment will shield an honest expression of opinion based either on true or privileged statements of fact. Both defenses, of course, fail if the public official proves actual malice, which a jury may pin upon the publisher even though the defense thinks the plaintiff has failed to prove it.

When criticizing a public official or figure the writer of the editorial to be printed or broadcast should:

    (i) know or in good faith believe the facts to be true; assume that an indication of possible factual untruth if not thoroughly double checked amounts to a reckless disregard of truth;

   (ii) state, fairly summarize, or make adequate reference to the facts upon which the criticism is based;

  (iii) if there is a factual libel, secure counsel's opinion that the writer has adequate evidence of truth;

  (iv) criticize in good faith—for the public good;

   (v) keep the criticism in the groove—official acts and public affairs; stay away from personal life unless clearly germane to the public affairs under discussion.

Criticism of Candidates

In discussions of candidates, the privilege should be the same as when a person already in office is the target. But be more careful. Apply the foregoing five caveats with even greater severity.

Criticism of Events of Great Public Importance

When criticizing an event of great public importance (such as foreign policy or inflation) it is not unnatural to name or identify persons. An "event" cannot be libeled, but the participants can. It is one thing to say that our policy favors totalitarian regimes. It is quite another thing to remark that an identifiable foreign officer sold out to a fascist government. If participants are torn to pieces the writer should be sure they are public officials or figures, and the comments tested against the five preceding guidelines.

CRITICISM OF PRIVATE VENTURES

Some private ventures are clearly in the public domain, others not. It must *not* be assumed that the privilege in respect to comment on public affairs extends to private affairs. Indeed, in Chapter 12 it will be seen that the right of privacy is being protected and extended.

When a person in private life is the target and the subject matter is personal, the facts on which criticism is based must be demonstrably true.

CRITICISM OF THE COURT

When the comments or story indicate mishandling of a juridical proceeding, there are three elements to consider: (i) possible contempt of court; (ii) the chance that excessive zeal on the part of the reporter or other inaccuracy has resulted in an abuse of the qualified privilege and consequent vulnerability to libel actions by counsel, litigants, witnesses, or third parties mentioned in the trial; and (iii) possible libel of the judge.

Most judges realize they are not set on a pedestal and decorated with a halo. They recognize judicial conduct should be an object of constant watchfulness and its judgments subject to the freest criticism.

Referring to human frailties and fallibilities, Mr. Justice

Felix Frankfurter remarked that: "judges must be kept mindful of their limitations and of their ultimate public responsibility by a vigorous stream of criticism expressed with candor however blunt." Speaking for the United States Supreme Court, Mr. Justice Hugo L. Black said: "And an enforced silence, . . . would probably engender resentment, suspicion, and contempt much more than it would enhance respect."

Often the most pungent critics of the opinions of a court are members of that very court. "This case is a shocking abuse of judicial authority. It is without precedent in the books," wrote three judges.

The severest criticism, well timed and properly expressed—that does not impinge upon a pending suit—is not a contempt of court. Nor will a judge as an individual have a cause of action based on defamation.

II. CRITICISM MAY BE SEVERE

Once established as proper, criticism may be powerful. Subject to the rules already discussed, the critic can write a philippic. He may condemn in no uncertain terms. He may use satire and proper invective, flanked by a cartoon.

Dismissing a complaint by Lord Tilkin that one of Lord Beaverbrook's newspapers had been overly rough, the Queen's Bench Division ruled:

> Any person is entitled to say, by way of comment on a matter of public interest, what he honestly thinks, however exaggerated, obstinate or prejudiced it may be. Such comment is fair and sustainable as a defense to a libel action unless it is so strong that no fair-minded person could have made it honestly.

Summing up, His Worship warned: "You should not misstate the material facts upon which you are commenting."

A book, for example, may be referred to as dull, shallow, and stupid, if the reviewer so believes. However, the review will not be protected as a fair criticism if the author is accused of plagiarism; that charge must be proved true.

Performers and musicians can be verbally crucified in respect to artistic competence, but usually not otherwise.

It should not be intimated that an athlete deliberately failed to do his utmost to win. Hints of payoffs or deals should be eschewed, unless the publisher is prepared to prove the truth or the announcement was made on an occasion of privilege.

In the gray area where it is unclear whether a certain organization or person is a proper subject of criticism, the criticism itself should be restrained and constructive, and the facts provably true.

A Checklist for Criticism

If there is a negative answer to any one of the following six questions, the proposed criticism should be reviewed again with possible libel especially in mind:

1. Is the subject of public interest or concern?
2. Are the facts upon which the criticism is based provably true or, in the alternative, clearly under the rule pertaining to public officials or figures and proceedings?
3. Must a fair-minded jury decide that the circumstances compel a finding that there was no malice or cavalier disregard of the truth on the part of the publisher— including the staff?
4. Is there an expression of opinion in contrast to an assertion of fact?
5. Is it a fair comment?
6. Is it in the public interest, free from the taint of malice?

SAY IT SAFELY

Libel based on comment or criticism almost always originates in a situation that could easily be avoided by use of
moderate journalistic skills. There is usually at least a little
time for reflection and verification—the deadline is not ten
minutes away. With care, stringent and caustic comment
and criticism may be made almost wholly safe—not safe
from threats of suit by disgruntled politicians and from occasional actual nuisance suits—but safe from verdicts in significant sums. The editorial which smacks of libel should
be read to counsel.

INVESTIGATIVE REPORTERS

Inherent in the product of an investigative reporter is a
special hazard. He unearths news in contrast to reporting
an undoubted event. Usually he would not be investigating
were it not for the prospect of uncovering crime or scandal.
His very diligence may lead to certainty on his part that he
has succeeded and there is no other side to the story. So
into his copy creep comment and criticism which may tran-
scend the provable facts.

The reporter may "know" many things to be true (which
in fact are true) but which cannot be proved to a jury by ad-
missable evidence. Under such circumstances, his comment becomes libelous. An investigative reporter must discipline himself to report only hard facts, free from his
opinion. He should not make a libelous assertion.

AD-LIB DISC JOCKEYS

The ad-lib radio and television broadcasts (including
"personality-type" disc jockeys who intersperse recordings
with comments upon the world and life in general) pose

CHAPTER 9

TRUTH, CONSENT, REPLIES, CORRECTIONS, AND RETRACTIONS

Nothing is so firmly believed as what we least know.

MONTAIGNE

Confession of our faults is the next thing to innocency.

PUBLILIUS SYRUS

I. TRUTH

Proof that the defamatory statement is substantially true is a complete defense to a civil action of libel.* "Justifica-

* Except in a few states which do not accept truth as a complete defense if the publication was from "malicious motives" or was "motivated by actual malice," or which require that along with truth it must be shown the publication was for "justifiable ends" or related to a "subject of public concern." Whether provisions of this type are unconstitutional will depend upon the subject matter of the publication. If about a public official or public figure, the *New York Times* rule will apply.

---

peculiar problems. There is little or no opportunity to check such remarks beforehand. Disc jockeys and all other ad-libbers must be schooled to keep their remarks within the rules of fair comment and criticism. Shop-talk programs are of the same class.

LIBEL OF GOVERNMENT

Government as such, as a massive apparatus, cannot be libeled. Strictures against "the Congress" or "the Army" or the "bureaucrats of the Agricultural Department" are too general to give anyone a cause of action.

The danger zone is reached when the editorial attacks a small governmental entity (school board, for instance) or a department of government under circumstances where an employee or official is able to demonstrate that, though unnamed, he has been identified.* If so, the defenses of privilege and comment will be available as when attacking public officials.

MULTIPLE CRITIQUES

It will be stressed that when there are several barbs and truth is the defense, substantial truth must be proved as to each. Similarly, if there is more than one criticism—whether different points or phraseology—the propriety of each criticism must be proved.

ILLUSTRATION

Plaintiff owned a private dock. By newspaper ads and otherwise he attempted to influence the city council and the public against construction of a competitive dock. By

* This is treated in Chapter 4 under the heading "Libel by Reference to a Class."

injecting himself into a matter of public concern and criticizing public officials, plaintiff invited comment and criticism leveled at him. Six alleged libels were brushed aside by the Supreme Court of Iowa. But the *Evening Democrat* let down its guard on the seventh.

It said: "There is no honorable reason for opposing a local boat harbor." The writer forgot that the antonym of "honorable" is dishonorable, shameful, unjust. Here the newspaper abused and (as treated by the court) lost its qualified privilege.

Though the court speaks of qualified privilege, this was a fair comment case where the newspaper made an unjustified criticism rather than a factual statement.

LOSS OF RIGHT—A REVIEW

The necessity of free and forceful comment, despite the hazards, is so great that a rephrasing of basic principles seems justified. The essentials of fairness are lacking in the following instances:

1. If the comment assaults motive, conduct, or character unrelated to the public matters to which the comment really relates.
2. If it criticizes a person's private life in respect to affairs unrelated to the public matter properly under discussion.
3. If it accuses a person of a crime or employs degrading or insulting epithets, except (i) when necessary or proper to show his unfitness for, or unfaithfulness in, public office, or (ii) when otherwise clearly appropriate to a legitimate end sought by a comment made in the public interest.
4. If the criticism is malicious—and a jury may infer malice from conduct.

It must be remembered that public policy does not require the protection of a person who, instead of expressing his honest opinion, seizes upon an opportunity to gratify h own malice or to exhibit his skill in vituperative utterance

CRITICISM REVERSED

A news broadcaster, or commentator assumes a dual rol of private citizen and public figure. While not an electe public official (an Ohio court remarked), his position must be considered analogous as far as criticism of his programs is concerned. His broadcasts are tantamount to a production or performance for public exhibition. Hence he submits them to criticism within the rules pertaining to fair comment. The same may, of course, be said in respect to all writers whose views are widely circulated.

tion" is a plea of truth. However, while the component parts of an article may be substantially true, if they are arranged in such a manner as to give the reader a false impression plaintiff may have a cause of action.

A reporter may "know" many things which he could not possibly prove in court. Hearsay and gossip are not admissible in evidence, even though everybody "knows" the statements to be true. For practical prepublication purposes, *a defamatory article should be presumed false unless it can be proved true by evidence which is admissible in court* and which will be available for the trial. It should not be published unless it is (i) provably true, or it is (ii) believed to be true and is clearly within the rules of qualified privilege or fair comment.

ILLUSTRATION

At a political gathering a candidate for public office shouts that his rival obtained his naturalization papers through perjury. It is easily provable that the story quotes the speaker accurately. But to sustain a defense of truth in an action brought by the rival, the publisher or broadcaster must go further and prove the perjury.

A mistaken belief in the truth of the matter published, although honest and reasonable, is not a defense unless the publication was privileged.

Fortunately, it is not necessary to prove that a story is meticulously true. Slight inaccuracies of expression are immaterial provided that the defamatory charge is true in substance. However the story must be a fairly complete factual statement. Publishing *part* of a suicide note (the attempt failed) was held a reckless disregard of the truth when the omitted portions would have given the readers a different impression.

MULTIPLE BARBS

Substantial truth must be proved in respect to each and every separate libel—every sting—in the publication. Otherwise a plea of truth (justification) fails as a complete defense. Then—possibly before a hostile jury under instructions from the judge—defense counsel will be confined to the contention that after all it was but a little libel. Yet if this little residuary libel is a libel per se, the jurymen can price it about as they please.

UNDERCUTTING THE DEFENSE OF TRUTH

If the principal justification is truth, a retraction may amount to an admission of falsity in circumstances where, if the admission had not been made, the defendant would have been able to prove substantial truth.

Insurance policies sometimes require the publisher to correct or retract the statement which is attacked as false and libelous. Occasionally they say "immediately." The insured must choose between (i) ignoring the terms of his policy, or (ii) hypocritically conceding that something is false though he still believes it to be true. The provision should be to this effect:

> If and when the Assured is informed that any person asserts that a false and libelous publication has been made concerning him (or her or it, as the case may be) the Assured will promptly investigate the claim and if (in the best judgment of the Assured and its counsel, if consulted) a retraction is in order, Assured will promptly publish whatever retraction or correction then seems appropriate in the situation.

The above is not an unfair or undue burden upon the carrier. It may save payment of a claim which probably would be pressed if falsity were admitted.

II. CONSENT

A person who consents to the publication cannot recover. As in the case of truth, consent means a consent which can be proved at the trial. The consent must be to the type of publication in question. If Joe College, class of '75, consents to the publication of a caricature and a supposedly humorous but scurrilous story in his fraternity magazine, he has not consented to a reprint in a publication of general circulation.

PSEUDO CONSENTS

Sometimes a person defamed in a proposed story readily grants an interview giving his version of the affair. *This does not in itself constitute a consent to publication of the defamation.* But, if he does not object to publication of the entire account as read to him, the interview is a significant factor when deciding whether as a practical matter the story, including his statements, may be run.

III. REPLIES TO ATTACKS

As between adversaries in the public forum, there is a considerable right of self-defense. When an individual has been attacked by, say, a political opponent, he may wish to reply through the medium which carried the original attack. Hence, even though the reply is defamatory of the original attacker, a broadcaster or publisher may have a qualified privilege in disseminating the reply, if the new defamatory matter is essential to support a contention that the first attack was unjustified.

Because the libelous reply is usually in response to a libelous accusation, the publisher or broadcaster could be in the midst of one libel already uttered and another potential. If he refuses to pass along the reply to the public, the injured party will claim connivance and malice. But if the reply is beyond what is necessary to answer the original attack, the originator will wail. The statutory position of the broadcaster of political material is considered in Chapter 14.

A danger is that the retort may not be responsive to the attack or may be stronger than is proper. Ordinarily, one must not shoot to kill an unarmed man when the present danger is no more than fisticuffs.

ILLUSTRATIONS

1. The plaintiff accused certain stockholders of a corporation of mismanagement and questioned their honesty. The reply called plaintiff a "shady" lawyer who kept clients' money and said his future status as a lawyer was in doubt. This was an irrelevant attack on plaintiff personally; the reply was not privileged.

2. The *Minneapolis Tribune* ran a story imputing malpractice to the plaintiff doctor. The defendant newspaper pleaded it was replying to a libelous article run the day before in another paper at the instance of plaintiff; it admitted the response was made in a moment of anger over the first publication. Because, as the court put it, there was time for "blood to cool," the first libel was not a defense to the libelous reply.

3. *Colliers* magazine accused a food processing company of intentionally conducting a false advertising cam-

paign. The food company fought back by saying that the magazine had prostituted the truth in its columns in an effort to force advertisers to buy space. A New York court found the reply responsive to the defamation by *Colliers*.

In some states remedial legislation may be an aid in defending suits stemming from replies to attacks.

IN PRINT VIS-À-VIS BY AIR

The statutory position of the broadcaster of political material is considered in Chapter 13. Equal time concepts come into play; the station is using publicly-owned airwaves under a license granted by the federal government.

The situation of the printed word is quite different. Florida enacted a "right of reply" law which gave a political candidate the right to demand free equal space to answer newspaper criticism of his personal conduct or official record. The Supreme Court struck down the statute because it violated the freedom of the press as guaranteed by the First Amendment (Chapter 19).

A voluntary "Right of Response" policy is not unknown. For example, the *Charleston* (West Virginia) *Gazette* guarantees that persons whose judgments and policies are challenged by editorials may respond at reasonable length and the response will be displayed as prominently as was the newspaper's own comment.

IV. CORRECTIONS AND RETRACTIONS

The importance of giving an accused person an opportunity to state his side in a story when it is first published or broadcast is emphasized elsewhere. Such an explanation may keep alive a qualified privilege which otherwise might be lost; it shows a desire to be fair and rebuts malice. Situations where falsity is claimed or suspected in a story already broadcast or published are somewhat different.

MITIGATION OF DAMAGES

Whether a correction or retraction should be made is a neat question of policy, depending upon all the circumstances and upon the law of the state where suit will be brought. About half the states have adopted statutes to the effect that a retraction may be introduced in evidence in mitigation of damages. A number of states limit recovery to actual provable damage unless a retraction is demanded and refused.

Other legislative safeguards to news media require that if he seeks general damages, plaintiff must plead and prove (i) that there was an intent to defame, or (ii) in the absence of such an intent, failure to retract upon written demand made within a specified time.

Statutory requirements vary. If publishing (communicating) in a state which enjoys legislation of this character, media should have detailed instructions from local counsel as to procedures to be followed.

EFFECT OF REFUSAL

Refusal to correct or retract a defamatory statement may be used to show malice or a callous disregard for the rights of others. Hence, when truth is not one of the principal defenses, a full and prompt correction or retraction is usually the better policy, although it is recognized that neither will ordinarily create a complete defense.

BE GRACIOUS

Whenever a correction or retraction is in order, it should not be grudgingly or ambiguously made. It should be full and frank, though it need not be abject. If printed, it should be published in as conspicuous a place as the article complained of. If the retraction is over the air and is incident to a serious libel which has attracted attention, some effort should be made to assure a listening audience greater than that which heard the broadcast. When possible, a rating should be made so that evidence tending to prove the number who listened to the correction will be available should it be needed.

A PRACTICAL HINT

Sometimes, *by agreement,* an affirmative story which makes no reference to the libel is a better solace to the aggrieved. *To illustrate:* The publication or broadcast defamed Jones by saying he was involved in a fraud. It may be possible to prove the story true; but that is not certain. Jones threatens suit for libel. If he, too, is not sure of his case, a pleasant story telling of his fine work in the Elks Lodge or of his daughter's wedding may satisfy him—without putting the publisher in an untenable position.

CHAPTER 10

CONTEMPTS OF COURT— REPORTERS' REFUSAL TO TESTIFY

If all printers were determin'd not to print any thing till they were sure it would offend no body, there would be very little printed.

BENJAMIN FRANKLIN

THE First Amendment to the Constitution of the United States says that "Congress shall make no law . . . abridging the freedom of speech, or of the press. . . ." Thus it guarantees against transgressing freedom of speech and of the press, now, of course, including other media.

The Fifth Amendment to the federal Constitution provides that "No person shall . . . be deprived of life, liberty, or property, without due process of law. . . ." Here is the guarantee of due process—a fair trial.

The Sixth assures an accused "a speedy and public trial, by an impartial jury." A public trial is a guarantee *to the ac-*

cused that he will be fairly dealt with and not unjustly condemned. History shows that secret trials are effective instruments of oppression.

Whether or not a state constitution has similar provisions, the Fourteenth Amendment, as now construed, makes these fundamentals (due process—public trial) applicable to state courts.

A public trial, then, is an ingredient of a fair trial. It becomes truly public because of news media, not by word of mouth originating with (usually) the handful who heard the trial. Pertinent constitutional provisions are quoted in Chapter 19.

RIGHTS AND RESPONSIBILITIES

Affirmative aspects of freedom of the press and freedom of speech are reflected in qualified privilege and the right of fair comment and criticism. Every right carries a corollary duty. The constitutional guarantees of free speech and a free press are expressly or implicitly subject to the burden that the speaker may be responsible for an abuse of his freedom. One manifestation of that responsibility is found in the law of libel; another in the right of privacy. A third segment is found in the rules pertaining to contempt of court.

This chapter has to do with contempts of court. Chapter 16 is dedicated to an overlapping but wider problem—the achievement of a reconciliation between the essentials of a fair trial and freedom to report to the public what goes on before, during, and after a trial.

SAY IT SAFELY

THE CONFLICT

Freedom of the press and fair trial are not in themselves the ends. Both are necessary adjuncts to the goal of freedom for the individual. Yet at times license to report court proceedings seems to clash with the judicial concept of a fair trial. The advent of photography and television accentuates the problem. The presence of reporters is accepted as a matter of course except for a few hearings which, as a matter of public policy, are conducted privately. Reporters sit quietly with pad and pencil.

Cameras and television equipment introduce a new element. Litigants, witnesses, lawyers, and even the judge himself may be camera-conscious or camera-shy. Many jurists believe that photographic activities within the courtroom make a fair trial difficult, if not impossible. Other judges now permit photography, usually only if both sides and the witness consent.

CONTEMPTS OF COURT

Any act which significantly derogates the dignity and authority of the court or which tends to impede or frustrate the administration of justice may be a contempt of court. The power to punish for contempt is inherent in the courts. This is deemed essential to the preservation of an independent judiciary and the protection of litigants.

As reflected in Chapter 8, the courts have no immunity from criticism. Under the rules there reviewed, anyone has wide latitude in honest though severe editorial comment upon the courts. Judicial inefficiency may be exposed. But a story or photo which tends (i) to produce an atmosphere of prejudice where a pending case is being or is to be tried; (ii) to delay or interfere with the administration of justice; or (iii) to cause justice to miscarry, may be held to be in contempt of court.

A case on trial is not an essential ingredient. Criticism of the law enforcement plans of an imperious judge, with "an excellent example of shotgun justice" as the punch line, resulted in a contempt citation to the editor and the posting of a $50,000 bond to avoid immediate commitment to the bastille.

Obviously the refusal of a reporter to testify as to his sources of information may impede or frustrate the administration of justice *if:*

> (i) in a criminal proceeding, the government or the accused has no other way of determining facts or sources of facts essential to the determination of guilt or innocence; of *if*
>
> (ii) in a civil case, after due diligence, either plaintiff or defendant is unable to unearth data or testimony essential to his case which might become available were the source of a reporter's story revealed.

The pressure put upon the reporter to testify is the possibility that the judge will declare him to be in contempt of court. Accordingly, the important subject of safeguarding news sources will be reviewed in this chapter concerning contempts.

TYPICAL CONTEMPTS

Critical editorial comment ineptly worded in respect to a pending suit is an obvious path to contempt proceedings. Perhaps the most frequent offense is playing up the opinions of detectives, alienists, and other experts, thus prejudicing a community and prospective jurors in advance of trial. While the case is being tried, publication of supposed facts not admissible in evidence may force the judge to grant a mistrial—here clearly interfering with the administration of justice. This may be so even though the jury is held overnight and theoretically has no access to the newspapers.

Other illustrations of possible contempts include:

1. Grossly careless or overdramatic handling of courtroom news.
2. Caustic cartoons depicting the trial.
3. Publishing or broadcasting stories about juvenile delinquents when forbidden by law, order, or rule of court.
4. Stories which interfere with the investigations of a grand jury.
5. Photographs taken in court against court rules or orders.

Even in the absence of a written rule, a judge has power to punish as a contempt any photographic expedition into his courtroom. As photographers who have been fined or imprisoned well know, the punishment is imposed by the very judge who believes that the dignity of his forum has been violated.

JUSTICE UNDISTURBED

Judicial decisions say that "the first requisite of a court of justice is that its machinery be left undisturbed." Hence, anyone who intrudes himself into the due and orderly administration of justice is guilty of contempt of court and subject to punishment.

Assume, for instance, a suit based upon permanent and deforming injuries to a five-year-old girl. The little girl has not been exhibited to the jury; she has not even been taken into the courtroom. A newspaper or newscaster describes her as a "bright and happy little girl" playing in the hall of the courthouse, "not at all depressed by her misfortune." In the courtroom the parents and their attorney are presenting their case under the theory that since the accident the little girl has been depressed and unable to join with her friends gaily in play as she did before the accident. *Query:* Would the news story constitute a comment on the evidence so as to interfere with the administration of justice?

When the Case Is Over

Most courts hold that comment on concluded cases cannot be punished as contempt—there might be a libel of the judge, though no contempt of the tribunal. However, occasional deviations say that a violent statement touching a concluded case may be a contempt. The rationale is that such a statement degrades the court and tends to destroy public confidence and impair the court's efficiency in subsequent litigation. Courts differ as to whether a case already tried and now on appeal, or one where the time within which to appeal has not yet run, is still pending or is over so far as contempt of court is concerned.

Reporters' Refusal to Testify

The reporter is usually on the front line, regardless of the medium used to transmit news to the public. But, on rare occasions, other personnel may become involved in the contempt of court stemming from the refusal. What if, under pressure on the stand, the writer blurts out: "The boss told me to protect my source."

Aspects ancillary to the specific testimony (or refusal to testify as to source) should be noted. The reporter must be present in court or before the grand jury to claim his privilege; he cannot refuse to appear. One reporter vainly contended that his mere presence behind the closed doors of the meeting room of the grand jury would destroy his credibility with his Black Panther Party sources.

However, there have been judicial intimations to the effect that a reporter should be able to resist a subpoena if he is able to show:

(i) bad faith attempts by a prosecutor to harass him and disrupt his relationship with his news source; and

(ii) the information he is being asked to give bears "only a remote and tenuous relationship to the subject of the investigation" or if he has "some other reason to believe that his testimony implicates confidential source relationships without a legitimate need of law enforcement."

Reporters who witness a crime must testify as to what they saw and heard. Questions concerning whether the reporter had observed firearms or explosives and whether their use had been discussed at a subversive meeting must be answered.

The illustrations just given involve more than source alone; the reporter himself observed activities and overheard plans. Where the inquiry is limited to source—"who tipped you off?"—the court may or may not sustain the reporter. No definite formula binding on all courts has as yet been spelled out. A good statement comes from the Supreme Court of Vermont. The reporter was asked to reveal his source of information respecting a drug raid. The Court decided:

he is entitled to refuse to answer unless the interrogator can demonstrate to the judicial officer appealed to that there is no other adequately available source for the information and that it is relevant and material on the issue of guilt or innocence.

In neighboring Massachusetts the result was otherwise in a libel suit brought because the *Wall Street Journal* defamed a contractor. The newspaper refused to reveal its source. The court held it to be the duty of reporters to appear, as do other citizens, with written material when required, and to answer relevant questions.

Actress Judy Garland prevailed over columnist Marie Torre. Ms. Torre wrote that an unnamed CBS executive thought Judy overweight. An indignant Judy sued for libel. She quizzed CBS executives. All denied saying such a thing. The court ruled it went "to the heart" of Judy's claim and ordered Ms. Torre to testify.

In one of the Watergate cases, counsel representing the Committee for the Reelection of the President attempted to subpoena photographs, tapes, and newsroom working papers from sundry newspapers and magazines. The subpoena was quashed because of failure to show that other sources of evidence had been exhausted. But what would the result have been if there had been a strong showing that every other avenue of information had been fully explored?

SHIELD STATUTES

Media yearn for the day when "shield statues" will protect reporters. It may be long in coming. The ideal, they naturally feel, would be a federal statute bottomed upon the First and Fourteenth Amendments to the Constitution, obligatory on all courts, state and federal.

The American Newspaper Publishers' Association has prepared drafts for Congressional consideration, one affording absolute privilege. Passage cannot be predicted. About half the states have enacted shield statutes. The practical protection afforded a reporter in a particular situation depends on the judicial interpretation of that statute in relation to the evidence before him.

Typically, a shield statute may protect representatives of media from being compelled to disclose the identity of a source of information except in course of an actual trial and then only after it has been established by clear and convincing evidence that:

(i) the disclosure is indispensable to the proof of or defense against the offense charged in a criminal case, *or*

(ii) to the proof of plaintiff's cause or defense against it in a civil cause, *and*

(iii) the evidence (often identity of an informant) cannot be obtained elsewhere, *and*

(iv) there is a compelling public interest in requiring disclosure of the identity or information.

Studies searching for the best way to express a sound social policy in protecting reporters' sources and information have proliferated. There are differences of opinion *within* the judiciary and the legal profession. The necessary caveats here are two: except in extreme circumstances, a reporter should not promise absolute confidentiality to a source unless (1) management has told him that media counsel has advised that in controlling jurisdictions the judge is bound by a law which protects a source, and (2) the publisher and reporter are both willing to risk the incarceration of the latter. (Excellent books and articles have been written by gifted men in dungeons!)

No certain precepts of universal application can be spelled out. Each situation should be reviewed and decided in advance. Factors include: law of the jurisdiction or jurisdictions (multistate coverage in print or through the air); confidence in accuracy of source; importance of story to the public; value of story to circulation or Neilsen rating; potential adverse court result of attempting to withhold source if litigation against media based on libel or violation of the right of privacy should ensue.

So in the present posture of the law, whether or not a reporter goes to jail for contempt rather than reveal his source will be a decision which is a mingled result of his own convictions and courage, the backing given him by his employer, and his attorney's advice as to the law of the jurisdiction. In many instances, but certainly not in all, counsel representing media will be able to work out an accommodation with those who demand the information.

Truth Not a Defense

The truth of a story is not a defense against a citation for contempt. If an unseemly editorial disparages the court, perhaps the truth hurts most. Punishment may be by fine, or imprisonment, or both.

Possible contempts are not everyday problems, as are incipient libels and violations of the right of privacy. Neither writers nor administrative personnel can be expected to develop an adequate discretion in respect to contempts—not even the courthouse reporter can do this. As an officer of the court, your attorney will sense the situation.

Demand a Subpoena

Even in controversies where the reporter is willing to testify, he should usually insist that he be served with a lawful subpoena (i.e., not appear "voluntarily," but under compulsion). Then he will not seem to be an investigator, volunteering his aid to a litigant.

Sometimes a prospective source will be satisfied with the promise: "I will not reveal to anyone that you told me this, *unless* I should be subpoenaed and the Judge orders me to answer."

CHAPTER 11

PICTURES—STILL AND MOVING

A room hung with pictures is a room hung with thoughts.

SIR JOSHUA REYNOLDS

As already shown, contempts of court may stem from the taking of pictures. Violations of the right of privacy are as often predicated on the picture as on the story. Hence, photographers are invited to consider the preceding and next succeeding chapters as well as this to be their special domain.

I. LIBEL AND PRIVACY

The fundamentals of libel apply to photographs and their captions. The privileges are essentially the same.

SAY IT SAFELY

Libelous Pictures

Error in identification is probably the most frequent source of libel based on pictures. Usually that is a "someone-blundered" situation. Perhaps years ago the picture was mislabeled in the morgue. Perhaps the writer of captions or cut lines made a mistake—excusable or otherwise. Not all libel based on pictures can be debited against photographers. But much of it can be, and most of that can be traced to careless identification. In contrast to script, which may be false, an accurately identified picture is in itself true.

Illustrations
Typical situations resulting in suits for libel include the following:

1. Picture of two or more persons at the jailhouse, the wrong one being identified as the character being booked.

2. Picture of "men mentioned" in the "blackmail scandal," plantiff not being singled out as an innocent bystander until near the end of the story.

3. Picture of a movie starlet in a scandal; wrong starlet or scandal.

4. Picture of one or a few out of many persons held by the police for questioning, captions giving the impression that some of those pictured are suspects, not merely potential witnesses.

5. Picture of the scene of an auto accident involving a crime, such as drunken driving, without making plain who are the accused and who are the injured innocent or mere bystanders.

6. Picture of a solid citizen erroneously identified as doing something amounting to any libel per se described in Chapter 3.

7. Feature story about customs inspectors, telling of their uncanny knowledge of hiding places, plus a picture

of identifiable persons passing through a customs inspection, thus suggesting that they are customs suspects.

Plaintiff had testified before a congressional committee as to how he had refused to take part in an alleged fraud. The *Boston Traveller* ran his picture with those of two other men under a banner headline: "SETTLEMENT UPPED $2000—$400 KICKBACK TOLD." No reference was made to plaintiff in the accompanying article. The court was unable to decide that as a matter of law there was *not* a libel per se. So the question was one for determination by the jury.

Among other principal roots of suits based on photographs may be listed:

1. Violations of conditions imposed by subject.
2. Retouching a picture to accentuate seminudity, however flattering the result may be.
3. Deleting part of the picture; superimposed or fake pictures; distortions and optical illusions.
4. Any picture accompanying defamatory text or cut lines.

When a picture is taken despite the objections of the subject, or when the photographer has shouldered his way into a private home or other unauthorized spot to take it, there may be a violation of the right of privacy. (See Chapter 12.)

CARTOONS AND SKETCHES

Sketches of current events are subject to the same tests as photographs. Cartoons are usually in the category of comment and criticism. They are subject to the rules of Chapter 8. Comic strips are mostly concerned with clearly fictitious characters. A few have created libel problems because of the use of the name of an individual.

Motion Pictures and Television

Newsreels are subject to the fundamental rules and gauges applicable to other media reporting current events. A play will be judged as would a published story. If it is based, or to the viewer appears to be based, on someone's life, a violation of the right of privacy or libel may enter.

The principles touching libel which apply to still photographs and text carry over to their ultimate—the broadcasting of pictures in motion plus accompanying sound. The picture broadcast must be judged in conjunction with what is said over television, much as the picture on paper must be interpreted in relation to the printed text.

II. Courtroom Photography

The taking of pictures (still, moving, or televised) during the course of a trial contrary to the rules or specific instructions of the court would likely lead to contempt proceedings against the photographer and his employer. To that extent, this is a proper subject for the preceding chapter.

News photography and television with the permission of the trial judge would not be a contempt. The question would be: Was there a fair trial? As to that aspect, the following discussion is a natural part of Chapter 16, "Free Speech—Fair Trial." But that chapter is concerned with all media.

Since this chapter specializes in photography, we bring the courtroom here.

Rules of Court

Believing that the taking of pictures in court is not fitting and results in improper publicizing of judicial proceedings,

most states—by rule of court or otherwise—have mandates
to the effect that:

> The taking of photographs in the courtroom, during ses-
> sions of the court or recesses between sessions, and the
> broadcasting or televising of court proceedings detract
> from the essential dignity of the proceedings and distract
> the witness in giving his testimony.

The precise wordings differ somewhat. Usually the rule
does not apply to a ceremonial such as a naturalization proceeding. The federal rules of criminal procedure are to the
effect that the taking of photographs in the courtroom during the progress of judicial proceedings or radio broadcasts
from the courtroom shall not be permitted. This federal
prohibition is commonly observed in civil trials.

THE TREND—MORE OR LESS PHOTOGRAPHY?

Before June 7, 1965, many newsmen who believed photography to be a desirable medium for reporting trials op-
timistically forecast that refinements in technology would
bring a relaxing of judicial opinion to the effect that court-
rooms must be forbidden ground for photography. Then
came the Billie Sol Estes decision by the United States
Supreme Court. It has three principal aspects: (i) its immediate impact upon televising criminal trials, (ii) other courtroom photography in criminal cases, and (iii) its probable
long-range effect upon photographing or televising.

TELEVISING CRIMINAL TRIALS

Splitting five to four, the court upset the conviction of
Estes because the trial was televised. The majority of the
court declared that "televising of criminal trials denies to

defendants their constitutional right of due process of law"—a fair trial. The opinion asserts that "experience teaches that there are numerous situations in which it might cause actual unfairness—some so subtle as to defy detection by the accused or control by the judge." Four possibilities were described in considerable detail; we can but list them:

1. Potential impact upon the jurors—deemed of the greatest significance.
2. The quality of testimony will often be impaired.
3. Additional responsibility the presence of television places on the judge. He must supervise an unnecessary distraction. He should not be put to the initial decision of whether or not to permit it, particularly in states where judges are selected at the ballot box.
4. It is a form of mental—if not physical—harassment of defendant, resembling a police line-up or third degree.

The Chief Justice begins his concurring opinion by agreeing that "the televising of criminal trials is inherently a denial of due process." He based his conclusion on three grounds:

1. The televising of trials diverts the trial from its proper purpose in that it has an inevitable impact on all the trial participants.
2. It gives the public the wrong impression about the purpose of trials, thereby detracting from the dignity of court proceedings and lessening the reliability of trials.
3. It singles out certain defendants and subjects them to trials under prejudicial conditions not experienced by others.

Four justices thought otherwise. "It is important," they said, "to remember that we move in an area touching the realm of free communication," and should "be wary of imposing any per se rule which, in the light of future technology, might serve to stifle or abridge true First Amendment rights."

In his concurring opinion Mr. Justice John M. Harlan wrote: "The Estes trial was a heavily publicized and highly sensational affair. I therefore put aside all other types of cases." It may be inferred that in a case involving less notoriety he might have decided differently. If so, only four justices voted to hold televised criminal trials to be constitutionally infirm, whatever the circumstances. Unless all parties and their counsel agree thereto, it is not likely that a trial judge will permit television in a criminal proceeding on the chance that the Supreme Court might decide that in his particular case there was no prejudice to the accused.

OTHER COURTROOM PHOTOGRAPHY IN CRIMINAL CASES

The Estes decision is built around television—an appendix includes seven full-page pictures of television gear. It should not be construed as erecting a constitutional ban against all photography, even in criminal cases.

However, as indicated, the Canons of Judicial Ethics bar the taking of photographs in the courtroom during sessions of the court or between sessions. Many rules of court are to the same effect.

Courtroom photography other than television has not yet been banned as *always* resulting in an unfair trial. If a particular judge clearly permits it, punishment will not descend upon the head of the photographer. But that judge may find his conduct challenged and in due course criticized by an appellate tribunal.

PROBABLE LONG-RANGE EFFECT UPON CIVIL SUITS

About the same may be said in respect to the trend in civil cases. An occasional judge will permit courtroom photography if all parties to the litigation agree and no witness objects.

The current formerly believed running in favor of courtroom photography has been reversed. Where it will stabilize, no one can foretell.

The Estes decision should be remembered as an example of the *kind of conduct* which invites restrictive court decisions and legislative bans. This comment applies to libel and right of privacy as much as to photography. Had the invasion of the courtroom and its environs by television been less flamboyant, perhaps the scales would have tipped the other way. The weight of one judge would have sufficed.

Except for this excursion into the courtroom, thus far libel and contempts have been the topics. Though a person libeled may be entitled to receive compensation for emotional distress resulting from the defamation, libel is primarily concerned with the individual's reputation in the minds of other people. Its main tests are external.

The right of privacy protects the individual's interest in freedom from emotional distress. Its tests are subjective, internal. We turn now to this kindred subject.

CHAPTER 12

RIGHT OF PRIVACY

> A newspaper should not invade private rights or feeling without sure warrant of public right as distinguished from public curiosity.
>
> Canons of Journalism of the American Society of Newspaper Editors

THE right of privacy—the right to be let alone—as increasingly enforced in the courts is a relatively new facet of the law. In 1890 Louis D. Brandeis and his law partner wrote an article, "The Right to Privacy." Denouncing the flamboyant journalism of that day, they contended that invasions upon privacy were subjecting individuals "to mental pain and distress, far greater than could be inflicted by mere bodily injury." They asserted that the press was "overstepping in every direction the obvious bounds of propriety and of decency." They discerned a common law right, "forged in the slow fires of the centuries," entitling a person to redress if his privacy was wrongly invaded.

Judges began to follow their reasoning; at least five*

---

* California, New York, Oklahoma, Utah, and Virginia.

legislatures took statutory notice of the problem. Today the right to be let alone, to be unmolested in private affairs, is recognized as legally enforcible in more than three dozen states.

I. AN EVOLVING RIGHT

Perhaps the trend of the times is best illustrated by an assertion in the Universal Declaration of Human Rights (1948): "No one shall be subjected to arbitrary interference with his privacy, family, home or correspondence, nor to attacks upon his honor and reputation. Everyone has the right to the protection of the law against such interference or attacks." There the new right against interference with privacy is named before the ancient right of redress for libel.

Though not all courts will follow it, and some scholars still challenge the very concept of a legally enforceable right of privacy, the April 1975 tentative restatement of the law of interference with privacy by the American Law Institute should be accepted as the currently most authoritative pronouncement. So while discussing general rules it will be followed rather closely in principle and clauses will be merged into the text.

From the viewpoint of the people talked about, many stories trespass upon privacy. "I wish that had not been in the paper." "We cringed when the news came over the air." But the publisher is not legally liable for violation of the subject's right of privacy unless the publication was unreasonable. Following the pattern of the restatement of the law pertaining to privacy, the judge or jury may find it so under any of the following circumstances:

1. The publisher or one or more of his envoys unreasonably intrudes upon the seclusion of plaintiff, his fam-

ily, or his private affairs in an effort to secure a story. Ringing the doorbell or knocking a suitable number of times and asking for an interview would not be an intrusion. But rudely insisting on an interview, backed by a photographer might well be. Pictures secretly taken of an unnewsworthy person might be adjudged a violation of his privacy.

Actions against publishers for violation of privacy based on a violent intrusion are rare; reporters and photographers are seldom that aggressive. But if and when it occurs, the publisher must remember that the *intrusion* is in itself a violation of privacy. Defendant publisher may be able to prove privilege and (if a violation is of a sort defined in paragraph 3 below) he may be able to establish truth, handily winning on those two facets. But as to the *intrusion,* the instructions of the judge may justify a verdict in plaintiff's favor . . . big enough, the angry jury might think, to cover the whole performance, intrusion, and subsequent publication.

2. Unauthorized appropriation of the name or likeness of another for business benefit. Here we are not talking of bona fide accurate current news stories. A feature article using names naively thought imaginary though actually the names of living persons (perhaps in the local directory), or a supposed news story pointing to the wrong person, or the unauthorized use of pictures may be actionable—particularly when exploited for commercial promotions. An unauthorized picture in an ad is the classic illustration.

3. When the published material is not of legitimate concern to the public and is of a kind which would be highly offensive to a reasonable person. A jury might be entrusted with the determination of whether the matter published (which the writer and editor thought funny, though perhaps a trifle off-key) would be highly offensive to a reasonable person. Again that dilemma—what is a "reasonable person?" Juries will differ; so good taste within the standards of the circula-

tion or broadcast area should be the foresight rule. A recent decision seems to justify the legalistic statement that anything which is a matter of public record may be published. However, as a foresight matter, personnel in the firing line should insist that management take the responsibility for publishing a defamatory record which is neither of immediate news value nor in the public interest.

4. If the subject of the story is placed in a false light highly offensive to a reasonable person and the publisher had knowledge of the falsity or acted in reckless disregard of the truth—perhaps even if he was merely negligent in his search for verity.

The last paragraph reads like a rule of libel. But like conditions 1, 2, and 3 preceding, it comes from the tentative restatement and when reread carefully and compared with a true libel, it will seem to require somewhat less than defamation, particularly per se. That of course broadens the risk to the publisher. A story within this formula might justify a suit under either or both theories—libel or violation of privacy. The plaintiff's attorney may think he will have a better chance to win the latter.

The "False Light" Theory of Privacy

A story which places plaintiff in a "false light" (an objectionable false light) is generally recognized as actionable. The scholarly general rule is condition 4, supra. It is particularly dangerous if the story contains inaccuracies and untrue statements. A story might be literally true, yet place plaintiff in a false light. "John was not drinking at the Red Wing Tavern prior to the auto accident." True. Also true: John is a teetotaler and had never visited *any* tavern. The very thought of a tavern is abhorrent to him. Was he libeled or his right of privacy violated?

Cosmopolitan magazine published an article entitled "Would You Wear a Monokini?" It contained a "cross-country survey" of women's responses to the question of whether the interviewee would appear on public beaches wearing a monokini. Upwards of forty opinions were printed; the names of the ladies quoted were given.

Plaintiff was one of them. She did not contend that the views attributed to her were either false or inaccurate. She did allege she thought her comments were casual and she had requested that they not be included in the article. The court held that the compilation was an accurate and nonfictionalized report of points of view on a matter of public interest. Under New York law plaintiff's right of privacy was not violated.

II. The News May Be Published

However, the situation must not be overstated. Certainly today's right of privacy does not prohibit publication and broadcasting of matters of public interest. The news may be made known and newsworthy pictures printed and broadcast even though the subject came unwillingly into the limelight. Following the language of the Supreme Court of Kentucky:

> There are times when one, whether willingly or not, becomes an actor in an occurrence of public or general interest. When this takes place, he emerges from his seclusion. It is not an invasion of his right of privacy to publish his photograph with an account of the occurrence.

Many persons are in themselves newsworthy. When a person becomes a public character, he relinquishes his right of privacy or at least great areas of privacy.

Working rules may be summarized by saying that the right of privacy does not exist where:

SAY IT SAFELY

1. The subject has himself published or broadcast the matter or has given provable consent—but consent or waiver can be rescinded before the broadcast or publication.

2. The subject is in the news because of his prominence or activities.

3. He is an object of legitimate public interest because of some event. However some judges speak of an area of privacy which may not be invaded with impunity even though related to the newsworthy event; for instance, a gruesome picture.

4. The subject is a corporation or public institution. *Caveat:* A strictly family type corporation might be an exception to this exception.

The right of privacy does not suppress the news or fair comments. However it is an aggressive defense against the publicizing of private affairs with which the public has no legitimate concern or the wrongful intrusion (the bad taste, if you please, of an intrusion) into private activities in such a manner as to cause mental suffering, shame, or humiliation to a person of ordinary sensibilities.

STALE NEWS

May a person, once in the news, by lapse of time reacquire a right of privacy as to his past life? A child prodigy, a failure as an adult, sued the *New Yorker* because of an unvarnished factual account of his life. The court denied recovery; there was a certain continuing public interest in what he had turned out to be.

An ex-convict sued NBC because it televised a dramatized fictional version of his conviction for murder and later pardon. He was not identified. There was no actionable invasion of privacy. But a former prostitute who had metamorphosed into a respectable matron was successful in a suit against the publishers of the unsavory incidents of her past. The California court found a constitutional right to "pursuing and obtaining safety and happiness."

Contrary to plaintiff's request, the *Los Angeles Examiner* published a story concerning the third marriage of a former city attorney and political figure. It told of "hectic times" during his career, including unpleasant details. The court held that this did not constitute a violation of his right of privacy.

DANGEROUS PICTURES

Courts have given consideration to a theory denominated a "relational right of privacy." This means, for instance, the right of parents to be spared suffering from the publishing or broadcasting of pictures of a son (not himself newsworthy) killed under grotesque or disgraceful circumstances. A story of a deformed, stillborn baby, plus a picture taken without the consent of the parents, ended in a judgment against the publisher.

Held to create a right of action were:

1. The picture of a husband and wife in an affectionate position as part of an article on "Love"—held not warranted by news value or the public character of the twain.
2. A photograph of a child as she lay in the street after an auto accident as part of a later safety-first article entitled, "They Asked to Be Killed." Original publication of the picture as news was not a violation.
3. A photograph of a female taxi driver as an illustration in a libelous article directed against taxi drivers in general. Plaintiff was not mentioned by name or otherwise identified.

4. Too vivid cheesecake (photograph or television) in relation to the sensibilities, vocation, and environment of the subject.

Three months after the event, a magazine ran an erotic story concerning the killer of plaintiff's husband, a policeman slain in line of duty. It was entitled, "If You Love Me, Slip Me a Gun." The publisher claimed the article was a factual account of the escape of a dangerous criminal, the heroism of law enforcement officers, and the eventual triumph of justice. The court disagreed, saying that the story "makes a strong appeal to the idle and prurient." The widow's picture was used. She had a good cause of action against the magazine.

In another action against the same publisher it was held that the widow and children of a man who had been kicked to death by a gang of adolescents could not recover for invasion of their privacy by an accurate factual account, illustrated with their pictures, three months after the homicide.

The two decisions are not necessarily in conflict. The "Slip Me a Gun" story was sensationalized. It was not news. The story of the juvenile delinquents was accurate and three months after the event the court thought it still had current news value. But this was a borderline case; three months is quite a while. The court might have decided otherwise. The story was not worth the fees of the defense lawyers plus the time of publisher's personnel spent preparing for and attending the trial.

PUBLIC EVENTS

A person attending a public event may be televised, or his picture may be taken as part of the audience. Someone who is traveling or is in a public place cannot object to being pictured as part of a general scene. For instance, a television camera "panning" the audience might televise a recognizable individual. But, without his consent (unless he himself is newsworthy), he should not be featured in a close-up shot. The lady with him may not be his wife.

Discussing "the area of privacy which may not be invaded even in this modern era of television," the Court of Appeals of New York said:

> One traveling upon the public highway may expect to be televised, but only as an incidental part of the general scene. So, one attending a public event such as a professional football game may expect to be televised in the status in which he attends. If a mere spectator, he may be taken as part of the general audience, but may not be picked out of a crowd alone, thrust upon the screen and unduly featured for public view. . . .

If, however, an individual is a public personage, or an actual participant in the public event, or if some newsworthy incident affecting him is taking place, his picture may be played up to its full news value.

ILLUSTRATIONS

1. An innocent actor in a great tragedy, whether limited, as a murder in his family, or widespread, such as flood, fire, or earthquake.

2. A deliberate exhibitionist, such as a provable public attempt at suicide—window ledge, for instance.

It is hoped that the apogee has been reached when an attorney representing a marine returning from the wars felt justified in bringing suit because a paper published a picture of him taken at the dock while he was weeping on his mother's shoulder. The theory was that the picture was an invasion of his privacy and humiliating to a hardy marine.

Would it be a violation of the right of privacy to mention that a person who comes into the public eye for a moment (such as deflecting a pistol aimed at the president) is a homosexual? The assertion is factually correct but not too many people including members of his family know of the eccentricity.

Not many years ago this would have been a libel per se—but defendable as a libel because true. Now it may or may not be a libel; but as a foresight matter, assume that it is.

COMMERCIALS

As already indicated, when advertising is involved the rule is more strict and, in some states, there may be a misdemeanor.

A violation may stem from the unauthorized use of a name or picture in advertising without an otherwise objectionable connotation. All of the following were so held:

1. Plaintiff was photographed in a store. Without her consent, her photograph was published to advertise the business.
2. Without her consent, a picture of the plaintiff—doubtless beautiful—was used in a cosmetic advertisement.
3. Displaying plaintiff's picture in an ad and stating he was a policyholder with defendant life insurance company.
4. "Before" and "after" pictures of plaintiff in trunks purporting to show his development before and after taking a physical improvement course. Ten years before he had proudly given consent to the use of the pictures. The second run, without a renewal of the permission, was an invasion of his right of privacy.
5. The War Department released a photograph showing

Reed as a member of a team of optical experts engaged in repairing lenses at the front. Reed had no right of privacy against the army's use of his picture in furtherance of its policy in building home-front morale. But this gave no license to an optical company to use the picture for advertising its wares. Reed's right of privacy was violated.

RESURRECTING THE DEAD

As in the case of libel of a person deceased, there is no actionable invasion of the right of privacy by penetrating the affairs of the dead if the living members of the family are let alone.

ILLUSTRATIONS

1. The widow and Sonny Capone sued because of a telecast depicting the notorious career of the gangster. They were not pictured or referred to in any of the broadcasts. Sonny had been a boyhood friend of the president of Desilu Productions and had begged him to refrain from producing "The Untouchables."

One of the three judges of the Court of Appeals found defendant's conduct "reprehensible" and that the "profit motive outweighed any concern about injury to innocent people." Reluctantly, he agreed that the widow and son did not have a cause of action for invasion of right of privacy.

2. The *Saturday Evening Post* used the title "Highway Robbery" with an article telling of bribery and dishonest construction practices during the building of federal-aid highways in New Mexico. Plaintiffs' deceased father had been the contractor. They claimed invasion of their right of privacy. They were not mentioned in the article.

The United States Court of Appeals recognized "a right to seclusion, [and] to freedom from public disclosure of personal matters of private life." But analogizing to defamations, the decision was that the action does not survive the death of the party whose privacy was invaded unless the complaining party's privacy was also invaded.

III. Defenses to Privacy Actions

The law is in a period of evolution or confusion, put it whichever way you wish, in respect to defenses to actions based on violation of the right of privacy. Freedom of the press (the First Amendment) has been brought to the ramparts and supports the publisher. Unfortunately the boundary where an action based on libel is no longer tenable yet a violation of privacy still exists, is impossible to demarcate precisely.

A most useful workaday rule is to be extra careful of *feature* stories involving people not in themselves newsworthy and not at the moment involved in a truly newsworthy event.

The dwellers of a sordid slum may seem to welcome a reporter and a cameraman who tell them they are producing a series to help clean up the ghetto. They pose and are interviewed. Filth and rats are described by an able reporter. The pictures are vivid, deserve a prize. Then those portrayed assert the series was sensationalized and sue for the violation of the privacy of their humble homes. Twenty-three people once did in a single suit.

Truth Not a Solid Defense

A picture which clearly violates a right of privacy may be a true picture of plaintiff. Provable truth may not be relied upon as a defense where right of privacy is concerned. Nor is absence of malice a complete defense. Plaintiff need not prove special damage. Hence, in that respect, a violation of the right of privacy is akin to a libel per se. Punitive damages have been allowed.

PRIVILEGE

Some authorities say that the rules pertaining to conditional privilege discussed in Chapters 6 and 7 are reliable defenses against an action based on violation of privacy. But as a matter of prepublication foresight, *that should not be assumed to be so* in the absence of approval from counsel after he has been told everything touching the development of the story and the taking of the pictures. It is difficult to think of a privilege to shoulder oneself through an unopened door of a home or into a private gathering.

Provable consent or a genuinely newsworthy event are the solid defenses. Even high public officials and private personages known worldwide may enjoy zones of privacy.

STATES DIFFER

It would be easy to arrange a neat tabulation purporting to list the fifty states and the District of Columbia in three classes:

1. Those which clearly recognize the right of privacy.
2. Those which are uncertain or vague.
3. The few which might be expected to deny it, but may change tune when the next case reaches that state's top court.

The variations, constantly subject to new decisions, are such that every publisher should have the opinion of his own attorney as to the status of the evolution of the right of privacy in his jurisdiction.

UNAUTHORIZED PUBLICATIONS

The term "unauthorized publications" is creeping into legal vernacular. Sometimes it may be pertinent when discussing a right of privacy situation. But even then it should be strictly limited. The right of privacy is violated because of what is said or pictured not *merely* because it was not approved in advance. Contents determine the case, not lack of acquiescence alone. Of course, if *provably* authorized plaintiff has no case.

The news columns and television and radio news broadcasts are rarely formally "authorized" except in news releases and interviews. Nor are editorials and comment on public affairs and personages. There would be little freedom left if "unauthorized publications" carried an infirmity simply because they were not sanctified in advance by all who might be touched by the story. A publisher or broadcaster should stoutly resist if and when liability is asserted against him under the theory that there was an "unauthorized publication."

A case against the *Washington Post* might be considered an illustration of an unfortunate unauthorized publication. Plaintiff was a twenty-one-year-old woman who had been raped. The story included her name and address. Responding to her claim for damages, the newspaper defended by arguing that she had become a public figure because involved in a newsworthy event.

But the judge ruled that the publication can be constitutionally protected only if (1) the matter is newsworthy and (2) it does not shock the community's notion of decency. He declared that the woman's name and address were not essential to the story, and that their publication deeply intruded on her private affairs. He said she did not *accede to*

publicity and the "extreme embarrassment that rape vic-
tims are commonly known to suffer coupled with the tender
age of the plaintiff weigh in favor of preserving her ano-
nymity." There are decisions to the contrary.

GOOD TASTE, THE ESSENCE

Courts have said that the right of privacy protects against
"the unwarranted appropriation or exploitation of one's
personality." The meaning and scope of that vague phrase
will be determined only when many more cases reach
courts of final jurisdiction. The preachment of this chapter
is: If publishers and broadcasters will exercise a modicum
of discretion and use the good taste which, as individuals,
they excercise in their own affairs, the now evolving right of
privacy will not become a greater menace. If it is given food
on which to grow this newborn right could become a Fran-
kenstein, deterring the publication or broadcasting of material which should be known to the public and which gives
news much of its human interest.

CHAPTER 13

RADIO AND TELEVISION

> *Zeal is very blind, or badly regulated,
> when it encroaches upon the rights of
> others.*
>
> QUENSEL

THE fundamentals of libel and of the right of privacy apply to communication by radio and television. In addition, broadcasters have unique problems. Some are inherent in their method of communication—broadcasts in contrast to the printed page. Others are created by fiat of regulatory bodies. The latter, particularly those resulting from the impact of the Communications Act of 1934 as amended and administered by the Federal Communications Commission in respect to political broadcasts, are reserved for the next chapter.

I. IN GENERAL

Though a newspaper's deadline may leave little time for deliberation, the editorial rooms do have an opportunity to read every word and scrutinize each picture before copy goes to press. In contrast, a broadcaster can never be completely sure that the script will be followed with fidelity, or that the television actor or speaker, by gesture or grimace, will not convey or emphasize a meaning not apparent in the words alone. Inflection of speech and gesture may carry as much or even more conviction than print or still picture.

In the absence of statutory relief, a station might be held liable for whatever it puts on the air, even though the utterance was a departure from script in defiance of instructions that forbid ad-libbing and in spite of seemingly adequate precautions taken by broadcaster's personnel.

DUE CARE

By common law reasoning some courts protected a station not at fault; but others did not. Most legislatures have met the problem by enacting laws to the effect that a broadcaster shall not be liable unless it is alleged and proved that he (meaning the station's staff) has failed to exercise due care to prevent the publication or utterance.

Whether the station exercised due care may become a question of fact to be decided by a jury. Failure to observe a libel per se in a manuscript submitted by a speaker or in a script prepared by the staff would almost certainly show lack of due care, whether the error stemmed from carelessness or ignorance. A station that permitted a person ignorant of the laws of libel to pass on copy would not be exercising due care. In short, the statutes do not relieve broadcast personnel from requirements of alertness comparable to those for journalists who communicate on paper.

There is not yet a body of case law from which can be gleaned rules clearly delineating due care. A speaker departs from his approved script—how many libelous words may he say before there is a failure in due care if he is not cut off? Or he makes small departures, each almost a libel or violation of privacy but not quite. Then, in one clause, before he can be cut off, he says something clearly actionable. Were small departures harbingers of the actionable statement so that in exercise of due care the station should have substituted a Strauss waltz?

As to writers of radio and television scripts, producers, directors, continuity editors, announcers, and all other station personnel, the proper caution is:

> Statutes ameliorating common law rules will help only if the broadcaster has been as careful as he can. The statutes will help defend if and only if due care has been exercised. So, as a practical matter, station personnel should be as informed, alert, and careful in states with protective statutes as in states without them.

Network Programs

Some statutes protect a station broadcasting a network program if it is not the station of origin. How such statutes will be construed in aggravated situations where due care would have prevented the tort is not yet known.

What Law Applies

State boundaries are no barrier to a broadcast. A court may hold that the final act of the broadcast occurred in a receiving set a thousand miles away, rather than in the studio. If a person resident and known in that distant state is defamed or his right of privacy violated, the law of that state may govern in the suit against the station. For this additional reason, therefore, except as to discretionary decisions by management, a protective statute should be thought of as a defense, not as justification for laxity.

II. Controversial Issues and the Fairness Doctrine

No legally qualified candidate is considered in this chapter. He will be a lead character in the next.

A newspaper, magazine, or book may be dedicated to the advancement of a point of view. Its field may be economic, religious, social change, partisan politics—or any its sponsor chooses. It can be biased and present but one approach.

Not so with broadcasting. Following the language of the Communications Act, the station has an obligation "to operate in the public interest and to afford reasonable opportunity for the discussion of conflicting views on issues of public importance." A station need not make its facilities available for controversial discussion of—say—the proposed freeway. But if it does, reasonable opportunity must be granted for the presentation of contrasting viewpoints. This is called the "fairness doctrine."

It imposes affirmative burdens on the broadcaster to provide fair coverage of issues of public importance—coverage which is adequate to inform factually and which fairly reflects differing viewpoints.

The rule is that when station time is granted for radio or television broadcasts concerning a controversial subject of public nature—any subject where opinions differ—the people on both sides of the question have a right to be heard. It matters not whether the program is commercial or sustained. Federal Communications Commission policy requires that a balanced presentation be afforded both sides. Whenever possible, the station should seek out the other side and offer time. Certainly, if equivalent time is requested, it should be made available if it is possible to do so.

Broadcasters must provide free time for the presentation of opposing views if a paid sponsor is unavailable. The basic principle underlying a broadcaster's duty to program balanced presentations on issues of public importance is the right of the public to be informed by or through those who are licensed to use the airwaves. It is not bottomed on a right of any governmental functionary or member of the public, or association of either, to broadcast their own particular views.

FAIR PLAY

Such are the requirements of fair play—the "fairness doctrine"—in the public interest. What constitutes fair play in a specific situation? That is the question. It cannot always be answered precisely, as in the case of statutory equal opportunity between legally qualified candidates—though even there, as will be seen, managerial discretion comes into play.

Some legal games have definite rules, easy to announce: Drive on the right side; a conveyance of real estate must be signed before a notary. Others are vague. "Reasonable." Just what does it mean when one must act "reasonably"?

The fairness doctrine cannot be reduced to a stencil. Once a controversial issue is put on the air, management must, in good faith, allocate time so that principal viewpoints can be brought to public attention. The good faith is exercised in the framework of inherent importance, public interest, pressure for air time because of other affairs which must be made known (war, earthquakes, politics, matters of great local interest, and so on), operational problems of the station, and all other factors which properly influence allocations of time. Perhaps it can be boiled down by saying: "Be intellectually honest, unswayed by personal preferences."

Non-Candidates

Unless a qualified political candidate is on the air discussing the controversial issue, the usual rules of libel apply, as modified by the statutes just described, which are designed to ameliorate the extra-hazardous situation of the broadcaster. The station may also be held for violations of the right of privacy or contempt of court.

Replies to Attacks

In Part III of Chapter 9 we touched upon reply to an attack as a defense to a libel action. It is the duty of a station to offer to those who are attacked an opportunity to answer the charges which have been hurled against them. But (except as to legally qualified candidates) the Communications Act does not grant the station exoneration from liability for libel incident to the reply.

Subject to available defenses, the station is responsible for the defamation present in the first attack. The station will be responsible also for libel in an offensive counter-offense, subject to the defenses discussed in previous chapters—with special emphasis on the duty of the station to furnish a forum for the reply. Script should have been read and corrected before the first libelous attack. The answer must be read and made safe, with the right of reply in mind.

Advertising

Broadcasters are not common carriers obliged to accept any commercial or (subject to the fairness doctrine and right to reply to personal attacks) any other advertisement. This is so even though the advertisement is offered on a cash-in-advance basis or by an advertiser of unquestioned solvency, and is free of libel and other legal infirmities. A *conspiracy* between media to refuse or limit certain types of lawful advertisements (used car dealers not simpatico with the orthodox new car agencies, for example) would be unlawful.

CHAPTER 14

POLITICAL BROADCASTS

In politics, merit is rewarded by the possessor being raised, like a target, to a position to be fired at.

BOVEE

A STATION is not required to permit the use of its facilities by any political candidate—more precisely, by the first to whom broadcast time is made available. But if the station grants time to one candidate, it must allow time to all who are running for that office.

The mandates applicable to broadcasts by qualified candidates differ in kind from the rules that apply to their advocates and all others.

I. BROADCASTS BY CANDIDATES

The Communications Act states that if a station permits any person who is a legally qualified candidate for any public office to use its facilities, equal opportunity must be afforded all other such candidates for that office, with no power of censorship over the material broadcast.

The requirements of the act as implemented by the Federal Communications Commission are such that a sharp distinction must be drawn between broadcasts by (i) a "legally qualified candidate" and (ii) anyone else. As to the former, the station may face delicate dilemmas in respect to possible libel. In extreme situations it may have to choose the lesser of two evils. Shall the first candidate be refused time on the station because of the risk that some of his utterances will be libelous or obscene, plus the risk—almost certainty—that rival candidates will demand an equal opportunity and perhaps retort in kind? Or should the station refuse all candidates for that office and endure the abuse that will follow each refusal?

Twice in the preceding two paragraphs reference is made to "that office." An indiscriminate or blanket policy of refusing time for all or several offices simply because of a dangerous candidate for one office, would not be in the public interest.

LEGALLY QUALIFIED CANDIDATES

If a station blandly assumes that every seeker of publicity who announces himself for office is within the statute, it may have to prove the truth of a scurrilous broadcast or pay damages to those defamed. Hence it is important to be able to distinguish between "legally qualified candidates" and those who are not.

Passing, for the moment, candidates for the presidency (or vice-presidency) of the United States, the status of a candidate must be decided in accordance with state and local law applicable to that election. In briefest form: A candidate is legally qualified if it appears that he will be on the ballot or will be put there by sticker or by writing in and be voted on in the coming election and, if elected, is eligible to serve.

When the candidate's name is not to be on the printed ballot, the station should not give him laissez faire as a qualified candidate unless it is clear he is making a serious race for the office. A candidate requesting statutory privileges carries the burden of proving that he is a legally qualified candidate. The station may make proper requirements in respect to proving qualifications.

PRESIDENTAL CANDIDATES

The nominee of the national convention of a recognized party is a candidate for president—or vice-president—of the United States. State and local requirements as to candidacies do not control—as they would in a mayoralty or gubernatorial election.

COMMUNISTS

Because of the provisions of the Communist Control Act, a candidate of the Communist party is not entitled to equal time. This rule may be changed.

> CAUTION
> Do not spread this exception to exclude a candidate of another party merely because he personally is or is thought to be a Communist.

OTHER CANDIDATES FOR THAT OFFICE

When a candidate demands time equal to that of the candidate who has been on the air, the station may require him to prove that he and his opponent are both "legally qualified candidates" for the same office or are rivals for nomination in the same primary.

Prior to convention or primary, the two or more parties are considered separately. Jones and Baldwin are both candidates for the Republican nomination, by primary or convention. If Jones is on the air, Baldwin is entitled to equal opportunity.

But Carrie, a candidate for nomination by one of the other parties, is not entitled to equal time; his is a separate race. Nor does time afforded a winning candidate in the primary *of itself* entitle his opponents in the final election to equal opportunity.

However, if the winning candidate in the primary of party AAA (and of course his opponent) were given dominant time while the primary candidates of party BBB were virtually off that station's air, in the final election between winner AAA and winner BBB, thought should be given before radically cutting both candidates. The end result of such a cut would be: the AAA candidate has enjoyed greater voter exposure during the primary while the BBB candidate has had relatively little exposure.

USE OF BROADCASTING STATION

If a candidate is permitted "to use a broadcasting station," all other candidates for the same office shall be afforded an equal opportunity. A 1959 amendment to the act helps define the meaning of "use." It provides that appearance on any

    (i) bona fide newscast or (ii) news interview;
    (iii) bona fide news documentary—if the appearance of the candidate is merely incidental to the presentation of the subject of the broadcast;

    (iv) on-the-spot coverage of bona fide news events—
        including political conventions and activities in-
        cidental thereto,

shall *not* be deemed to be "use." These helpful exceptions do not relieve management of the burden of exercising sound discretion in respect to the very broadcasts just listed.

The FCC held that to qualify under this provision: (i) the program must be a regularly scheduled program of the station or network in question, (ii) the determination of the content and format is made by the station or network and not the candidate, and (iii) the coverage was made by the station or network in the exercise of its news judgment and not for the candidate's political advantage.

Suppose a friendly newscaster questions the candidate at unusual length or the candidate becomes virtually unstoppable and pre-empts a disproportionate amount of time—has there been a "bona fide news interview"? If not, competitors must be afforded an equal opportunity. Or suppose the coverage of a news event results in one candidate being on the screen or his utterances on the air three times as much as his competitor? Five times? Ten times? At some point the bona fides of the newscast taper away and the lucky candidate is using the station instead of the station using him as an item of spot news.

Any use of the station not clearly within the listed exceptions should be considered a use, entitling the opponent to equal opportunity. Nor do the exceptions relieve a station of its obligation to operate in the public interest and to afford reasonable opportunity for the discussion of conflicting views on issues of public importance on the very broadcasts excepted from the equal opportunity mandate.

SAY IT SAFELY

WHO MAY SUE?

It has *not* been said that failure to afford equal time establishes a right of action on behalf of the disfavored candidate. Indeed, the opposite was held by the United States Court of Appeals in an action for damages ($25,000,000) brought by a disgruntled candidate for mayor of Chicago. The basic purpose of the act is regulation in the public interest and not the creation of private rights. Enforcement is by the Federal Communications Commission. It considers the broadcasting of political programs as a criterion to be evaluated both in license renewal proceedings and in contests for radio or television construction permits. And the reputation of the station may be affected adversely by plausible charges that it is giving a favored candidate extra time over the public's air.

NO CENSORSHIP OF CANDIDATES

The station may not censor—may not edit—the script of a legally qualified candidate. The station may not delete libel. The balancing factor is that the station is not legally responsible for defamatory or other improper statements (e.g., obscenities) by the candidate. A leading decision points out that if a station were not protected against suit the situation would be untenable, because "unless a station refuses to permit any candidate to talk at all, the [law] would sanction the unconscionable result of permitting civil and perhaps criminal liability to be imposed for the very conduct the statute demands of the station," and any rule to the contrary would be "in conflict with traditional concepts of fairness."

Secure Advance Copy; Reason Together

If the request is made of all candidates for the office in question, the station may require script in advance of the broadcast. If there is any doubt as to the good taste or emotional stability of the candidate, this may be a wise thing to do. The rule against censorship connotes denial of any examination of thought or expression designed to prevent (forbid) publication of objectionable material. Nevertheless, if it is made plain that there will be no censorship or forced deletions, management may reason quietly with the candidate and suggest that because of possible libel or other ill, he may wish to change the text. Perhaps he will quickly agree that it is good politics to do so. The conversation must be a soft sell. A promptly dictated log for the files is desirable; the candidate might later claim censorship.

Obscene Statements

Few candidates will intentionally include obscenity—it would alienate voters; nearly every candidate will follow a friendly suggestion to delete material which is in palpable bad taste. If he does not, and his opponent has used the station, he must be given equal time.

Forecast
Someday, over a nationwide hookup, an eccentric candidate will shock the public with vulgarities not related to campaign issues. Then the law will be amended to permit the station to delete that kind of trash.

Equal Opportunities

The station must "afford equal opportunities to all other" qualified candidates, not merely to the principal opponent of the one first on the air.

The equal opportunity need not be measured with scientific precision. The day of the week and hour need not be the same—indeed, an opportunity to the second or third or fourth candidate to reply quickly may be the essence of equality. Management must, in good faith, do its best to afford each candidate equally desirable time—as much of it to one as to another.

PRIMARY AND FINAL CAMPAIGNS

Though it is permissible to treat the primary and final election campaigns separately from the standpoint of equal opportunity, a broadcaster's obligations in respect to controversial issues might make it unwise to allow a drastic imbalance to occur. For instance: Suppose that during the primary campaign candidate Webster is permitted to purchase or is given ten hours of time, whereas candidate Green requests only two hours. It might be difficult to refuse a timely request by Green for more time in the runoff than is requested by Webster so that in the aggregate Green may have as much time as Webster had. Then of course Webster might counter by demanding equal time measured by the final election alone. If the station makes a genuine effort to be fair the dilemmas will probably dissolve—or be forgotten after election day.

NO CHANCE TO BE NOMINATED

Not every crackpot who announces himself as a candidate is actually a legally qualified candidate within the meaning of the act prior to the time he is on the ballot.

Nevertheless, it must be stressed that an announced candidate cannot be refused equal opportunity merely because all political prognosticators say his chances are nil. Somewhere down the line a delicate but genuine distinction must be drawn between a zealot making a hopeless race and a maverick making noise. The zealot may make the ballot and someday his views be accepted as sound.

ILLUSTRATION
   The mayor of a large city energetically sought the Democratic nomination for President in advance of the Democratic convention. Although he never had the backing of a significant number of the delegates, the FCC ruled that he was a qualified candidate. He convinced the FCC that he was making a bona fide race for the office by sending out brochures to all of the delegates from the various states, by having his name entered in one or two of the state Democratic primaries, and by rushing about and making speeches attempting to line up votes.

II. By Advocates of Candidates and Others

We have been discussing rights which are personal to candidates only. The statutory requirement of "equal opportunity" does not reach requests for time by political parties, as such, campaign committees, and articulate supporters. Nor does candidate Jones have a legal right to demand an equal opportunity because Smith, not a candidate, has spoken over that station against Jones or in behalf of a rival candidate.

Other Campaign Speakers

When the candidate himself is not the speaker, the station may treat the broadcast as it would any other controversial program. Advance script should be required; language which appears to be defamatory or obscene or which tends to invade the right of privacy should be stricken. If the integrity or emotional stability of the speaker is doubtful, adequate safeguards that he will stay by his script may be imposed. In short, the station can do what is fair under the circumstances and in the public interest, without needlessly exposing itself.

The fairness doctrine, already discussed, comes into play. In the Times-Mirror Broadcasting controversy, the FCC ruled that where the broadcasting station had permitted a commentator or other persons not a candidate to take a partisan position on issues involved in a race for a political office and to attack one candidate or support another by direct or indirect identification, the station must immediately send a transcript of the pertinent continuity in each such program to the opposing candidates and should offer a comparable opportunity for an appropriate spokesman to answer the broadcasts.

Utterances by Public Officials

The statutory requirement of "equal opportunity" does not apply to a statement made by an official before he becomes a candidate, even though he may be planning to run. After he becomes a candidate, the situation is different. It often requires a fine discernment to determine when that Rubicon was crossed.

When a Candidate Is Libeled

When a candidate thinks he has been defamed, he may—probably will—demand an opportunity to respond. If the attack was by a duly qualified candidate, the answer has been given in Part I preceding.

If the libel was uttered by someone else, the handling of time for reply and the contents of the reply come under the principles applicable to fair play summarized in Part II of Chapter 13.

The reminder is: If a station permits a legally qualified candidate to respond to a person who is not so qualified (e.g., a supporter of an opposing candidate), the facilities of the station must be open to all other qualified candidates for that office. The caution is that if any third person first brings the black cloud of libel into view, it may be better to refuse the air to all candidates for that office.

OFF THE SCRIPT

As a practical matter, it is almost impossible to prevent a reckless speaker from ad-libbing libel. A number of states have enacted legislation designed to protect the station (not the speaker) when the station has used due care as to the script.

PRACTICAL PROTECTION

A station wants no libel broadcast over its facilities even though it will not have to pay damages because of what a candidate says. As a practical matter, how can management protect itself?

1. Remember that the die is cast when an affirmative answer is first given.
2. In acute situations where serious libel would be a rational prognosis, deny time to all the actual candidates for a particular office.
3. Put the spokesmen for candidates on the air only after review of script and adequate assurance that there will be no departure from it.

4. In Chapter 5 under the heading "Practical Politics" the possibility of an indemnity agreement was suggested. As to advocates only (not a candidate) it may be useful here.

If after the broadcaster reasons with the candidate (without threat of censorship), there seems still to be danger but it is deemed advisable to permit the candidate to use the station:

1. Require him to submit by specified deadline either a full script or a complete outline of his talk.
2. Gently remind the candidate, his advertising agency, and, if possible, leading members of his campaign committee, that (though the station is exonerated) they may become involved in a suit based on libel or conspiracy if their candidate defames his adversary. His committeemen may be grateful.

A Record of Requests

Records of all requests for political broadcast time should be kept as required by FCC regulations. It is prudent to make a tape of all political broadcasts. Otherwise the station may be put to the difficult task of proving what was actually said in rebuttal to the testimony of friends of the man who claims to have been libeled.

CHAPTER 15

OBSCENITY
AND PORNOGRAPHY

Immodest words admit of no defence,
For want of decency is want of sense.

WENTWORTH DILLON

THE familiar language of the First Amendment to the Constitution of the United States, "Congress shall make no law . . . abridging the freedom of speech, or of the press," also restricts state legislatures and subordinate legislative bodies. As a result, a plethora of convictions for violations of laws inhibiting pornography and obscenity have been funneled to the Supreme Court of the United States for final decision. Sometimes they appeared in bundles. There have been so many cases that Mr. Justice Jackson is said to have spoken irreverently of the Court as the "High Court of Obscenity."

For a score of years, the Court has struggled for words which satisfactorily define the demarcation line between constitutionally protected freedom of speech and unpermissible public portrayal of obscene activities, whether by words or pictures.*

THE SEMANTIC EVOLUTION

We start from the constitutional base of freedom of speech. There is an unfettered right to the expression of *ideas*, regardless of how abhorrent they may be to the majority—the vast majority, if you please—of the people. But the public portrayal of lewd sexual activities, particularly when done for financial gain, is a different matter. In 1957, in a landmark decision commonly called the *Roth* case, the court plainly decided that obscenity laws are constitutional exercises of governmental police power. In the language of the court, the gist of the test for determining obscenity then was

> whether to the average person, applying contemporary community standards, the dominant theme of the material taken as a whole appeals to prurient interest.

Soon, in an effort to sharpen the definition of obscenity, Mr. Justice Harlan wrote that the federal statute requires proof of two distinct elements: (1) patent offensiveness and (2) "prurient interest" appeal. Both must conjoin before challenged material can be found "obscene."

Still we are left with subjective, individual judgments. "Patently offensive" may mean one thing to someone trained in a church school and something quite different to a product of the slums. The dictionaries more or less agree that the characteristic of "prurient" interest is addiction to

---

* *Caveat:* This chapter does not forecast the regulations and rulings of the Federal Communications Commission.

lascivious and lustful thoughts. But when does romance metamorphize into the lust which may not be pictured or described in defiance of a statute forbidding obscene writings and pictures?

Trying to resolve what Mr. Justice Harlan termed "the intractable obscenity problem," in a case originating in California, the Court held that the permissible scope of state regulation of obscene materials is constitutionally confined to works which depict or describe specifically defined sexual conduct and those which transgress the following guidelines:

1. Whether the *average* person [italics ours] applying contemporary community, not national, standards would find the work, taken as a whole, appeals to the prurient interest.
2. Whether the work depicts or describes in a patently offensive way, sexual conduct specifically defined by applicable law.
3. Whether the work, taken as a whole, lacks serious literary, artistic, political, or scientific values.

If the answers are yes the penalty may be fine or imprisonment or both. The Court candidly gave as examples of pornography transgressing the guidelines, patently offensive representations or descriptions of:

(i) intimate sexual acts, normal or perverted, actual or simulated, and
(ii) masturbation, excretory functions, and lewd exhibition of the genitals.

Nudity alone, without obscene connotations, (Venus de Milo) enjoys constitutional immunity. Perhaps not in conflict with the general rule just stated, a California trial judge castigated the American Civil Liberties Union and upheld a Los Angeles ordinance banning nudity appearing on the covers of publications vended from racks on the city's streets.

To summarize in other words: A work describing or picturing offensive hardcore sexual conduct may be forbidden even though it contains *some* but not "serious" literary, artistic, political, or scientific value. To be verboten, it need not be utterly without such values.

But still the peripheries are vague, and may vary from court to court and jury to jury. "Patently offensive" to Jones may be rollicking humor to Smith.

AN ELUSIVE NATIONAL STANDARD

Following the language of Mr. Justice Brennan, the Court has explicitly refused to tolerate a policy whereby "the constitutional limits of free expression in the nation would vary with state lines." He saw even less justification for allowing limits to vary with municipal or county borders. *In legal theory*, the constitutional status of an allegedly obscene production must be determined on the basis of national standards as set by the Supreme Court. The Justice noted: "It is, after all, a national Constitution we are expounding."

But except as to the proportionately few controversies which are ultimately decided by the United States Supreme Court, can this ever be so as a practical matter? Each of the hundreds of state judges and the thousands of jurors who briefly participate in the judicial process has family moral standards differing somewhat from all others.

Realistically, in the overwhelming majority of instances when an accused is brought into court and a judge or jury is to decide whether a statute forbidding obscenity has been violated, the decision will be by persons to whom "patently offensive," "pornographic," and "obscene" carry different meanings. To some, to take the name of the Lord in vain is a sin; to others, it is part of customary conversation.

Hence, when a proposed publication borders, even remotely borders, upon the obscene, the potential publisher must have in mind the mores of his circulation or listening area. In a conservative county in the Middle West an editor might be sent to jail for utterances or pictures which would be considered little more than frivolous in a highly sophisticated region.

The instructions of three trial judges in three separate trials, word for word the same, scrupulously following the then latest Supreme Court pronouncement setting forth the *national* definitions and tests, might lead to a "not guilty" verdict by one jury, a "guilty" verdict by another, and a hung (divided) jury in the third instance.

Advertising, Cover, and Headlines

Among other salacious items, Ralph Ginzberg published a book entitled *The Housewife's Handbook On Selective Promiscuity.* His attorney contended that the publications could not be outlawed under the then current (1966) definitions of obscenity. The Court bypassed this argument and turned to the advertising. Ginzberg's promotion was more important than the content of his books. The Court found that:

> each of the accused publications was originated or sold as stock in trade of the sordid business of pandering—"the business of purveying textual or graphic matter openly advertised to appeal to the erotic interest of their customers."

SAY IT SAFELY

A dictionary helps on the meaning of "pandering"—to supply clients for a prostitute or to supply women for illicit intercourse.

The overaggressive Ginzberg sought to postmark his publications from Intercourse, Pennsylvania. Failing there, he settled for Middlesex, New Jersey. He was convicted by his advertising methods and cover displays rather than by the text of the author. Sales activities condemned the whole.

Headlines to stories might do the same. And certainly advance promotional material concerning, say, a coming series entitled "Confessions of an Understudy" might weigh the scales in favor of the prosecuting attorney if criminal proceedings were brought against the editor of the newspaper or magazine or program on the air.

Conduct versus Contents

The court later earmarked three channels which might make the marketing of otherwise passable material a criminal act: (i) enticing juveniles with titillating texts and pictures, (ii) distribution of obscene material in such a fashion that it violates a person's privacy because of the practical impossibility of avoiding exposure to it (bold ads in a publication or a billboard), and (iii) sales made in a pandering fashion, as in the Ginzberg program.

The impossibility of slide rule definitions of obscenity which will enable judges and juries to be consistent in their decisions as to *content* of the material claimed as obscene, may justify a forecast that adjudications may tend to lean even more heavily on advertising and marketing methods than in the past. If a purveyor of obscenity and pornography seeks to attract buyers by touting the lascivious content of his product, perhaps he should be taken at his word and be convicted of violating laws forbidding obscene publications.

JUVENILES

The court draws a distinction between sales to juveniles and to adults.

Likewise legislation prohibiting obscenity may distinguish between what is lawful for vending to juveniles in contrast to adults. But the statutes must spell out fairly precise standards so that the administrators have an objective approach when deciding what may be tolerated and what forbidden. Door to door sales may be prohibited.

PRIVACY

As has been seen, risqué but passable contents may be made criminal by the marketing methods used. Blatant advertising may add to the transgression by trespassing on the privacy of the reader or hearer. If pornography thrusts itself before the eye or into the ear under unexpected circumstances, almost unavoidable by the recipient, it may be judged differently than, for example, if found in a frankly racy magazine.

A newspaper or periodical vended for family reading does not enjoy the pornographic freedom of a "girlie" magazine. The privacy of the home might be violated by an objectionable text—perhaps no more pornographic than Chapters 7 and 8 of the Songs of Solomon readily readable in the King James version or *The New English Bible.* A startling, prurient ad in the theater section of a newspaper might be found unlawful, in part because it unexpectedly, without invitation, invades the privacy of the home.

NEWSRACK PORNOGRAPHY

The United States Supreme Court had before it a Jacksonville, Florida ordinance making it a public nuisance and a punishable offense for a drive-in movie theater to exhibit films containing nudity when the screen is visible from a public street or place. The ordinance was not restricted to sexually explicit nudity; it referred to all nudity, however innocent or educational. The court struck down the ordinance as an invasion of First Amendment rights (Chapter 19).

The decision may be of interest to circulation departments in respect to newsrack legislation. Pedestrians can ignore a newsrack just as passengers in a car can ignore a drive-in movie screen. Bringing equivalent nudity into the privacy of the home by television might lead to a different result.

PRIVATE POSSESSION

In 1969, overruling the courts of Georgia, the Supreme Court upheld the right of a person to possess privately—not to circulate or publicly exhibit—obscene pictures.

CHAPTER 16

FREE SPEECH—
FAIR TRIAL

For many years, lawyers and news media have been battling each other with vehemence and vigor.

DEAN ERWIN N. GRISWOLD
Harvard Law School

THE current conflict in viewpoint in respect to news coverage of trials—before, during, and in some instances after—is of major significance. At one end of the spectrum are those who believe the best interests of society are served by rules which afford news media the utmost latitude. At the other end are those who are convinced that present freedom in reporting trials must be drastically curtailed.

The First (free speech) and the Sixth (fair trial) Amendments to the federal Constitution are said to be on a collision course. (See Chapter 19.) There are proposals to muzzle media. The most intense clash of opinions originates in the field of crime, particularly the coverage of pretrial news. Before attempting guidelines in reporting events incident to arrest, accusation, and trial, we must picture the opposing positions as best we can. This is not an easy task. Bench and bar are not of one rigid conviction. Policies of publishers differ sharply. The most that can be done here is to report what is believed to be the consensus, then survey the best marked path.

Those who deal in news must remember that the courts have the final say. They may order and penalize. So first comes the consensus of bar and bench, the operational personnel of the law.

I. A Fair Trial

Conduct by personnel of news media that results in punishable contempt of court is discussed in Chapter 10. Here we are concerned with stories of trials which:

(i) media management believes should be published in the public weal, or are at least permissible;
(ii) judges and lawyers may believe make a fair trial impossible;
(iii) under the circumstances, are not a contempt of court in the conventional sense—i.e., there may be a mistrial, but no serious contempt proceedings.

There may be a valid analogy between libel compared with right of privacy on one hand, and contempts compared with good taste in reporting news of trials on the other. Beyond the law of libel there is an increasing tendency on the part of the courts to protect the right of privacy, which means punishment of media for bad taste that injures someone. Beyond punishment for contempts as heretofore spelled out, there is a searching for formulas to prevent publication of matter deemed prejudicial to a fair trial— which again means bad taste in view of the potential trial of a man who is presumed to be innocent.

The Attorney General of the United States has issued a statement of policy applicable to personnel of the Department of Justice. It says that "certain types of information [news] generally tend to create dangers of prejudice." They are:

    (i) observations about a defendant's character;

   (ii) statements, admissions, confessions, or alibis attributable to a defendant;

  (iii) references to investigative procedures, such as fingerprints, polygraph examinations, ballistic tests, or laboratory tests;

  (iv) statements concerning the identity, credibility, or testimony of prospective witnesses;

   (v) statements concerning evidence or arguments in the case, whether or not it is anticipated that such evidence or argument will be used at trial.

Personnel of the department may make public:

    (i) defendant's name, age, residence, employment, marital status, and similar background information;

   (ii) the substance or text of the charge, such as a complaint, indictment, or information;

  (iii) the identity of the investigating and arresting agency and the length of the investigation;

  (iv) the circumstances immediately surrounding an arrest, including the time and place of arrest, resistance, pursuit, possession and use of weapons, and description of items seized at the time of arrest.

Such is the viewpoint of the most important law office in the land. As a canon of conduct, it applies only to the Department of Justice. However, as a studied expression of legal opinion, its reach is broader. Certainly, in many situations, there will be a duty (and if not a duty, a right) to publish much more than lawyers and law enforcement officers see fit to release for publication. Nevertheless, the standards which members of the bench and bar set for themselves are important when determining the policy question of what should be published. In Part III of this chapter we will see promulgations where the varying viewpoints are reconciled and brought within one cover.

The New Jersey Supreme Court believes that unfair and prejudicial stories before and during trial of criminal cases are becoming more and more prevalent. The onus is spread upon publishers, lawyers, and law enforcement officers. The court interprets the Canons of Professional Ethics as banning certain types of statements to news media by members of the bar—alleged confessions; inculpatory admissions by the accused; that the case is conclusive against the defendant; references to defendant's prior record of arrests or convictions and *also* statements respecting the innocence of the accused.

Writing in the *Trial Judge's Journal,* Mr. Justice John J. Francis of that court calls upon trial judges to enforce the rules of ethics. Trial judges countrywide were told that for some eight months New York papers "had been filled" * with the accounts of the murder of two young women. When a suspect confessed, a police officer made the public announcement that "We wouldn't have booked him if we weren't sure . . . we got the right guy, no question about it." News media carried the quotation and the circumstances surrounding the confession. The confession turned out to be untrue.

> It is hard to believe [the Justice said], . . . that if Whitmore [defendant] had gone to trial a jury could have been drawn which would not have included persons who had read or heard about his confession. Could such persons really remain uninfluenced by the damning pretrial pub-

* *Query:* Does the use of the word "filled" meet the standard of accuracy expected of newsmen when reporting crimes?

licity? Would any cautionary admonition by the judge, no matter how strong, really vitiate the effects of such publicity? Fortunately, Whitmore has not had to stand trial. It now appears that he is innocent, and that his confession was not true.

The eminent Justice concludes:

> Liberty of the press cannot be invoked in support of acts which invade the domain within which the authority of the courts is exclusive. Legitimate interests of the press do not require that encroachments on the right to fair trial be sanctioned. If courts abdicate their responsibility in this area, not much can be asked of the news media.

Another issue of the *Trial Judge's Journal* lists eleven "current activities working toward a satisfactory solution of the problem." The problem and the searching for the solution will be in the foreground for many years to come.

II. Free Speech

The Press-Bar Committee of the American Society of Newspaper Editors concluded that the claim of prejudice to fair trials by news coverage is "not proven"—is but a theory, not a fact. A plank of the committee is that a democratic community is not merely *entitled to know* promptly the facts about crime and the administration of justice, it *must know* them, else the very functioning of our government is endangered. Pointing to the need of intense and continuing public scrutiny, the committee said:

> A large part of the administration of justice in this country operates within, and is a part of, a political system: many judges, prosecutors and sheriffs are elected officials, subject to all the political pressures, good and bad, that characterize our democracy. If that part of the system

is to operate successfully, another part, the press, must exercise without fetters both its responsibility for watching the administration of justice and its freedom to report what it observes.

Granting that it is too many if even a handful of defendants is denied a fair trial because of prejudicial publicity, the committee cited statistics indicating that instances of prejudicial result in relation to the bulk of criminal cases are trivial in number.

The committee had assessed "the feasibility of the principal restrictions that are common to most of the proposals made by concerned members of the bar and bench." The committee was convinced that "the repressions entailed by those proposals would not only cause a forfeiture of the public's credence in their news media but would withdraw the essential safeguard of public awareness and scrutiny from the processes of justice."

Stressing the need for continuous public scrutiny of the courts and the administration of justice, the committee was firm to the effect that if the press is to perform its functions, it "must not be bound by the same regulations that govern the operation of the law enforcement agencies and the courts." The committee was persuaded that "no set of specific rules can be written into a code of press conduct that will not do more harm that good."

This ASNE report concludes with an excellent statement of principles for consideration by the Fourth Estate. Media should:

(i) rededicate themselves to the principle of reporting criminal affairs with restraint, good taste, and scrupulous regard for the rights of defendants, including the presumption of innocence, fair treatment, and fair trial by unprejudiced jurors;

    (ii) reaffirm their obligation to provide the public with full, objective, prompt, and honest information about criminal affairs, law enforcement, and the administration of justice;

   (iii) reject as impractical and harmful, attempts to restrict necessary news coverage by rigid regulations unduly limiting reporting of criminal and legal matters or suppressing information about them;

   (iv) undertake with open-mindedness and sincerity frequent discussions with the law enforcement agencies, the bar, and the bench, at all levels, for the purpose of creating mutual understanding of the problems involved, correcting abuses, resolving complaints, and furthering both full news coverage and fair trials.

Here and elsewhere we have given more lineage to "fair trial" than to "free speech." The latter is in the blood of all who gather and process news. The necessity of a fair trial as seen by judges and lawyers is less familiar ground. Both are essentials to a free society, though if forced to choose, Thomas Jefferson might have said that from the standpoint of preserving freedom for all citizens the few who unjustly are accused of crime must bear the risk of publicity that may be prejudicial (or perchance beneficial *) to their cause.

Starting with the premise that the opinion of the people is the basis of our government, Jefferson remarked: ". . . were it left to me to decide whether we should have a government without newspapers, or newspapers without a government, I should not hesitate a moment to prefer the latter." "But," he added, "I should mean that every man should receive those papers, and be capable of reading

---

* In California, in a suit against a manufacturer of drugs, plaintiff argued that he was denied a fair trial because news media ignored the trial. Lack of publicity, his attorney pled, gave the jurors the impression that the case was of minor importance.

them." Had Jefferson been writing 175 years later, perforce he would have included the new media.

An analogy is found in privilege, absolute and qualified.

1. Public welfare requires that upon some occasions the innocent may be defamed maliciously and the lie repeated without redress to the injured.
2. Protection against crime and unjust imprisonments requires that steps leading to, as well as occurrences during and after a criminal proceeding, be subject to examination by the electors; this is another way of saying "be in the news," when the proceeding is considered newsworthy by someone other than officialdom.

Both 1 and 2 impose sacrifices upon an occasional innocent citizen who finds himself in the line of fire.

We now turn to more specific recommendations by study groups in respect to reporting crimes.

III. A FAIR BALANCE

Divergent viewpoints and approaches have been summarized. Significant facets are these:

1. Media must admit many instances of flamboyant sensationalizing of trials—principally criminal, some civil. It is no wonder that judges and lawyers often feel a fair trial to be impossible.
2. Lawyers, defense and prosecution, and law enforcement officials must admit that all too often they feed the flame of excessive publicity and enjoy its light.
3. Consistent with the philosophy of the highest court in the land, the judges recognize that the courts must be open to public scrutiny—star chambers are not our way of life.
4. All groups want fair trials illuminated by free reporting so that the citizens will know that justice is evenhanded.

In approximately half the states the bench, the bar, and the Fourth Estate have worked together through joint committees to develop statements of principles or guidelines for the use of public officials, judges, media management, and on-the-firing-line personnel in this critical jousting field. Massachusetts, North Carolina, Oregon, and Washington are among those which have been in the forefront. When working out the "Free Press–Fair Trial Principles and Guidelines" for the state of New York, there was direct participation by twenty-two organizations and principal publishers plus five "observers" including the three broadcasting associations.

Rather than quote from state guidelines and point out differences, it seems well to utilize the 1973 "Composite State Voluntary Fair Trial–Free Press Agreement" laboriously developed by the Legal Advisory Committee on Fair Trial and Free Press of the American Bar Association.

If their product seems unduly long, pray remember: (i) the problems are many and complex, some stimulating emotion rather than reason, and (ii) some state pronouncements are even longer. Just as I believe every lawyer should reread his Code of Professional Responsibility and Canons of Judicial Ethics at least annually, so I suggest that all those touched by the dilemmas faced in the following Composite Agreement should review it periodically— except, of course, in those states where adequate guidelines have been spelled out. Then those should be reread.

PREAMBLE

In order to promote better understanding among the news media, the bench and bar, and law enforcement agencies in their efforts to support the Constitutional guarantees of freedom of the press and of fair and impartial trials, the following Statement of Principles, and

SAY IT SAFELY

Guidelines for the Reporting of Criminal Proceedings, have been mutually formulated by representatives of the organizations signatory to this agreement. They are submitted for voluntary compliance and recommended to all members of these professions in the State of _____.

STATEMENT OF PRINCIPLES

1. We respect the co-equal rights of a free press and fair trial. We believe that the principles set forth herein, if applied responsibly and in accord with high professional ethics, will help assure fair trials without limiting freedom of the press.

2. The public is entitled to have through the news media as much information as possible about the administration of justice, excepting only information that impairs the ends of justice or the rights of citizens as individuals. Members of the bench, the bar and the news media should cooperate, consistent with their respective ethical standards, in accomplishing these ends.

3. All parties to litigation are entitled to have their causes tried fairly by impartial tribunals. Lawyers and journalists share with the court responsibility for maintaining an atmosphere conducive to fair trial.

4. The news media and the bar recognize the responsibility of the judge to preserve order in the court and to conduct proceedings in a manner that will serve the ends of justice.

5. Decisions as to handling of news rest with editors, news directors, and reporters. In the exercise of news judgments based on the public interest the editor, news director and reporter should remember that:

(a) an accused person is presumed innocent until proved guilty;

(b) readers, listeners and viewers are potential jurors or witnesses;

(c) no person's reputation should be injured needlessly.

6. Members of the bench and bar should, within their respective codes of ethics, cooperate with the news media in providing information about law enforcement and the administration of justice. However, no lawyer should exploit any medium of public information to enhance his side of a pending case. It follows that the prosecuting attorney should avoid taking unfair advantage of his position as an important source of news. This shall not be construed to limit the prosecutor's obligation to make available information to which the news media and the public are entitled, as set forth in the Guidelines that follow. The same obligation applies to law enforcement officials.

7. Journalistic and legal training, both academic and on-the-job, should include instruction in the meaning of Constitutional rights to a fair trial and to freedom of the press, and the respective roles of the bench and bar and the news media in guarding these rights.

GUIDELINES FOR THE REPORTING
OF CRIMINAL PROCEEDINGS

The bench, the bar, law enforcement agencies and the media must exercise good judgment to balance the right of the public to be informed and the right of the accused to be protected against the release of prejudicial information prior to trial. The following guidelines are intended to assist in decisions to achieve such a balance.

1. It is appropriate to make public the following information for publication at the time of or immediately following an arrest:

(a) the accused's name, age, residence, employment, family status, the facts and circumstances of arrest and the length of the investigation where appropriate, a description of items seized and whether there was resistance or use of weapons;

(b) to announce the identity of the investigating and arresting officers or agency, the substance or text of the charge such as complaint, indictment, information and, where appropriate, the identity of the complainant;

(c) such information as may be necessary to enlist public assistance to apprehend fugitives from justice, or to protect the public from danger.

2. The release and publication of certain types of information may tend to be prejudicial without serving a significant function of law enforcement or public interest. All concerned should be aware of the dangers of prejudice in making pre-trial disclosures of the following types of information, which lawyers for the prosecution or defense are forbidden by the Code of Professional Responsibility from releasing publicly:

(a) opinions about an accused's character, guilt or innocence;

(b) admissions, confessions or the contents of a statement attributed to the accused, except that a lawyer may announce that the accused denies the charges against him;

(c) references to the results of any examinations or tests, such as fingerprints, polygraph examinations, ballistics or laboratory tests;

(d) statements concerning the credibility or anticipated testimony of prospective witnesses;

(e) opinions concerning evidence or argument in the case, and whether or not it is anticipated that such evidence or argument will be used at trial; or

(f) prior criminal charges and convictions, although they usually are matters of public record. (Their publication may be especially prejudicial immediately preceding trial.)

3. When a trial has begun, the news media generally may report anything done or said in open court. They should consider very carefully, however, publication of any matter or statement excluded from evidence outside the presence of the jury. This type of information may be highly prejudicial, and if it reaches the jury could result in a mistrial. This precaution is especially important in instances when the jury has not been sequestered for the duration of the trial.

4. Law enforcement and court personnel should neither encourage nor prohibit photographing or televising of defendants in public places, other than in the courtroom or immediate environs. The taking of photographs should not be otherwise restricted by judicial orders except as may be necessary to preserve orderly trial processes. However, persons in custody should not be deliberately posed for photographing or televising, and press interviews should not be granted unless the accused person requests an interview in writing, or consents to the interview after being informed of his right to counsel and his right to refuse to grant an interview.

CONTINUING CONSULTATION

We recognize the desirability of continued joint efforts to resolve areas of difference that may arise in our mutual objectives in protecting the correlative rights of freedom of speech and press, and fair trial. We recommend that designated representatives of the respective organizations signatory to this agreement meet periodically to consider questions of interpretation of the guidelines and their application to specific situations; also, to receive, evaluate and make recommendations with respect to complaints and to seek through educational means a proper accommodation of the correlative rights involved. We recommend further that educational seminars be held on state or regional levels as a means of continuing education among lawyers and newsmen, and that annual reports be issued to summarize results of the agreement as well as to identify particular problems which arise.

SAY IT SAFELY

The American Society of Newspaper Editors and the Radio Television News Directors Association cooperated in the development of the Composite Agreement. Obviously it does not automatically replace agreements and rules of court already in effect. But it should prove a handy guide to workers in states which have not yet promulgated and distributed guidelines, and to those striving to polish and perfect voluntary agreements already adopted—some a decade and a half ago.

The Composite Agreement has to do with criminal charges and trials where problems most often arise. Guidelines have also been developed for the reporting of juvenile court proceedings, civil proceedings, and the reporting of public records. They are available in the *Fair Trial/Free Press Voluntary Agreements* handbook, one copy of which will be furnished without charge by the Legal Advisory Committee on Fair Trial and Free Press, American Bar Association, 1155 East 60th Street, Chicago, Illinois 60637. A meticulously prepared study entitled "Free Press and Fair Trial" sponsored by the American Newspaper Publishers Association will be of particular interest to counsel representing media. This study is also available from the ANPA, 750 Third Avenue, New York, New York 10017.

As in the case of related problems of publication (measuring libel; qualified privilege; possible violation of right of privacy), the answers to questions incident to reporting trials distill to common sense, good taste, and judgment applied (i) in the framework of the facts of a particular case, and (ii) with the fundamentals of free speech and fair trials in mind. "Always" and "never" are words too strong for application here.

In recurrent situations, media cannot be expected to publish the meager account appropriate when a suspect is apprehended in a routine crime. Sometimes the importance of the accused or of the victim makes the crime a *cause célèbre*. Occasionally the very enormity of the crime—plus, perhaps, eyewitnesses, quick capture, and a confession—make a major story a must. In many a situation responsible media can scarcely suppress what is already known by word of mouth or from a publisher who plays up criminal news. There may be a duty to publish facts to counteract rampant rumor.

A decision that, in a particular instance, criteria applicable in most cases are inapplicable and that the crime should be reported with more than usual detail, should not be made lightly. Management should have in mind:

1. Possible libel—qualified privilege destroyed by excesses—see Chapter 7. (He may be found not guilty!)
2. Possible contempt of court—see Chapter 10.
3. Will the detailed story anger the judges and thus increase the pressures toward undesirable restrictions?
4. Is the story in the public interest?

The fundamental is—is the story unfair to either the accused, who is presumed innocent, or to the prosecution, which is charged with safeguarding society from the criminal element?

CONFESSIONS

Subparagraph 2(b) of the Composite Agreement refers to confessions.

Courts are holding that an accused has an absolute right to a full hearing on whether a confession he has signed was given voluntarily. If the judge rules it was a voluntary statement, it becomes admissible in evidence. If not truly voluntary, it will not be revealed to the jury.

SAY IT SAFELY

Herein lies one of the knottiest problems. During the investigation period of a criminal case, media can (and sometimes do) withhold the news that the accused has signed a confession. If a juror has learned of the confession, he has learned it through other channels. (In a small town almost everyone might "know" of the confession except—apparently—media, which say nothing about it!)

Then comes the trial. In open court, but in the absence of the jury, the question of whether the confession was voluntary may be determined. If channels of communication are closed to jurymen, the fairness of the trial will not be affected. But if stories are published telling of the conflicting evidence in respect to the confession and these stories reach jurymen, obviously the defendant may be prejudiced, even though the confession itself is not admitted into evidence.

Whether media should ever agree not to publish what has been said in open court is a debatable question. In some places the hearing in respect to the validity of the confession is held prior to the trial itself, media withholding stories of that hearing. The results of this program are similar to those obtained when the hearing on the confession is delayed until the trial has begun, then the jurors are isolated so that they will have no knowledge of the stories published covering the evidence introduced while they were locked in the jury room.

It Could Happen Here

In England permissible news of criminal proceedings is strictly limited. In France freedom to report on judicial proceedings is threatened by a relatively new code of penal procedure. Police, magistrates, and lawyers may not reveal details of any criminal case; the public prosecutor or magistrate may make a written statement in order to negate "misleading news."

There are stirrings within some state legislatures. A maverick bill was introduced in a midwestern state which, if passed, would have imposed stringent criminal sanctions to prevent publication of anything except that the arrest has been made and, later, information admitted into evidence at the trial. It would not be a defense to the publisher that the news story had "no prejudicial effect on the trial," or that the story was true.

The best policy is to keep an even keel, avoiding the excesses which tempt retribution harmful to all, including the accused.

IV. JUVENILE COURTS

Philosophies and policies in respect to reporting proceedings in and ancillary to juvenile courts vary from alpha to omega. At one extreme are those who are convinced that there would be fewer youthful crimes if they were more generally reported and names given. Dramatic decreases in juvenile felonies are claimed for areas where juvenile hearings are open and participants usually identified in the news. Data favorable to open hearings are, however, challenged by investigators from social agencies.

At the other extreme are those who believe that to label a boy as a miscreant may mark him for life. The tendency will be to hurt rather than to deter. They say that some escapades are motivated by a desire for attention—publicity will encourage rather than discourage wrongdoing.

The nub of the divergence in viewpoints may, perhaps, be described another way. Those who favor publicity assert that the fine Oriental tradition of family responsibility will be furthered if the ignominy of one member of the family be visited on all. Families will see to it that their children behave if it is well known that the clan name will be shamed if they do not.

A SAMPLE OF OPINION

A survey was conducted by the *Wenatchee Daily World.** Responses were from a fair sampling of law enforcement officers (70), newspaper editors (113), juveniles (601), and the general public (278)—all in the Pacific Northwest. Of all adults, 84.5 percent believe that publicity helps reduce juvenile delinquency. Juveniles voted 49.5 percent "yes" and 50.5 percent "no."

Only 15 percent of the adults said that publicity encourages juveniles to commit offenses; only 26.9 percent of the juveniles agreed with them—73.1 percent of the juveniles believe that publicity does *not* encourage crime.

Of the juveniles, 47.5 percent favored publicizing even the first offense if grave and 98.3 percent favored publicizing second offenders. The adult vote was 97 percent in favor of exposing the second grave offense and 76.1 percent for the first.

Sixty-five percent of juveniles would publish the names of all traffic offenders; 83 percent of the adults would do so.

There is a middle ground. Its tenets are stated in "Guides for Juvenile Court Judges in News Media Relations," promulgated by the National Council on Crimes and Delinquency. An advisory council of judges from twenty-eight states sponsored the report. It recognizes that the juvenile court is an integral part of the judicial system. Therefore, the public has a right to know:

* This paper won a certificate of merit in the American Bar Association's 1965 awards program "for outstanding published articles contributing to public understanding of the American system of law and justice."

 (i) the basic principles under which the court functions
     and the manner of its operations;
 (ii) the kind of staff the court has;
 (iii) the degree of the court's success or failure and the
       reason therefor;
 (iv) the kinds of problems the court deals with day after
      day and the *impersonal* facts of cases which may il-
      lustrate these problems.

The report thus recognizes that the court has an obligation
to make certain information accessible to news media—but
it uses the word "impersonal."

Asserting that news media and judges should work
together with confidence in, and respect for, each other, the
council laid down guidelines to which, they believe, juvenile courts and news media can subscribe:

1. News media should be welcomed to all sessions of the
   juvenile court.
2. Responsibility for developing sound public interest in
   and understanding of the child, the community, and
   the court must be shared by the judge and the news
   media.
3. All official records should be open to the news media
   with the judge's consent, unless inspection is prohibited by statute.
4. Confidential reports should not be open to inspection
   by the press, except at the express order of the court.
5. The judge, *at his discretion,* may release the name or
   other identifying information of a juvenile offender in
   his court.
6. The court should strictly adhere to the Canons of Professional Ethics, which generally condemn the release
   of information concerning pending or anticipated judicial proceedings.
7. If an act of delinquency is publicized, news media
   should be informed of the disposition of the case.

Again we see an approval of withholding of news by the judge—"at his discretion" names may be released.

Such are the recommendations to the judges and to the members of the Fourth Estate, released in April 1965. The sponsors are students of the problem, most of them with a wealth of practical experience. Whether, after ten or twenty years have passed, the best judgment of a similar group will be the same, only time can tell. There are constant changes in the philosophy and practical approach of educators in their field and social workers in theirs. Pediatricians run through phases—four hour feedings, three hour, two hour, whenever the baby is hungry as nature intended, and then, *presto,* back to four hours. Similarly, the results of over-much secrecy and protection against publicity (a natural concomitant of crime) may impel the resurgence of the belief that adverse publicity deters crime, and does not encourage exhibitionists as some now say.

Obviously, the quoted recommendations do not have force of law and are not binding except as, coincidentally, one parallels the statutes or local rules. Newsmen should find them helpful (i) in showing star-chamber-minded judges the error of their ways, and (ii) in deciding what news of juvenile misbehavior and punishment is in the public interest. Certainly the tragedies of children haled into juvenile court should not be exploited for sake of circulation or Nielsen ratings. Equally certain is the fundamental that there are occasions when the facts should be told and the participants identified regardless of the current recommendations of workers in that vineyard or the preferences of a judge—unless of course the publication is contrary to law or would generate a contempt of court.

Subject to statutory restrictions in respect to publishing

stories concerning the perpetration of offenses by youth, there is a wide scope for editorial discretion. In a large city it may be deemed useless or even harmful to publish names as a matter of course. In a nearby town, news media may be convinced that, with occasional exceptions, it is a public service to publish names. Depending on the local situation and tradition and the personalities involved, the geography may be reversed. In the smaller community it may be thought best not to let the neighbors know more than they learn by word of mouth, and in the city the publicity may be deemed an instrument of law enforcement. And in either area a wave of juvenile delinquency may change what was once deemed a firm opinion.

Implicit in the quoted report is the recognition that, as stated by John Henry Wigmore in his description of the modern juvenile court:

> Privacy of examination of the delinquent and his family is . . . regarded as generally useful and occasionally essential; and the statutes usually provide for this.
>
> But insofar as . . . practice habitually exercises the power [of strict privacy], it has its [risks]. No court of justice can afford habitually to conduct its proceedings strictly in private.

Again, a great scholar of the law implicitly recognizes media as a handmaiden of justice, "an indispensable element," as phrased by Mr. Justice Frankfurter.

Since many who believe in minimum reporting of juvenile court proceedings would, in effect, ultimately put control of the news to be released (not direction as to what should be published *) in the hands of the judge, the opera-

* Some zealots seem to favor giving the judge supervisory discretion over what may be printed.

tive result of their philosophy would be a secrecy inconsistent with public surveillance of the workings of an important branch of the judicial system.

However, the specter of an occasional star chamber, dominated by a judge unsuited to his assignment, must not distort the day-to-day picture. Most of the judges presiding in juvenile court are dedicated to their baffling task. They will recognize news as a necessary adjunct to the judicial machinery of a free society. They will cooperate with newsmen who show understanding of the overall problem. When, in a particular situation, a difficult decision must be made, it should be made on the basis of public good.

It has already been mentioned that some of the voluntary fair trial–free press agreements suggest guidelines for juvenile coverage. And there are statutes and rules of court which may not be disregarded with impunity.

CHAPTER 17

DANGER ZONES

> *If a little knowledge is dangerous, where*
> *is the man who has so much as to be out*
> *of danger?*
>
> T. H. HUXLEY

CHECK and double check. Usually any one of several men could have corrected the error, or at least recognized the possible presence of defamation and referred the copy to someone for verification or scrutiny. When dealing with defamatory matter not clearly privileged or easily proved true, it is prudent: (i) to double check the facts; (ii) to do so in such a fashion that every juror will say, "The writer and, in fact, everyone handling the copy did everything they could to be careful"; and (iii) when proofreading and processing, to handle like an explosive.

CRIMES

Stories concerning crimes are apt to be libelous per se of someone, if untrue. As cautioned in Part I of Chapter 7, until a charge is filed, circumstances do not ordinarily warrant more than a statement that the police are holding whoever it may be for questioning in connection with the crime of which a story tells.

To say, "Blank was jailed on an open charge" may convey to the public the impression that a charge of some sort has been filed. "Blank was not charged but is being held," or "Blank is held in jail but has not been charged," is more accurate. Statements of this sort are justified because provably true. However, there are times when the nature of the crime or the prominence of those involved requires much bolder treatment. Under those circumstances, the responsibility of the source, the reputation of the accused, and all other factors must be weighed and a sound discretion exercised.

In any such story a denial of guilt should be as conspicuous as the accusation.

COLUMNISTS

Data are not available, but it is doubtless safe to assert that syndicated columns and columnists are involved in a disproportionate number of libel actions. A mathematician might say that the hazard of libel is in inverse relation to the distance. A column refers to someone resident in, say, Denver. As a practical matter, the story might be safe enough in any state other than Colorado, plus perhaps nearby areas of adjoining states. Before publication or broadcast a column should be read in the light of the local situation. If, despite the risk, a possibly libelous statement regarding local people is to be published, they should be given a chance to answer, preferably in the same issue, just as though the story had been written locally. The last item in this chapter headed "Wire Stories" applies here.

CRUSADES

A crusade series is vulnerable because the stories are not founded on spot news brought in through ordinary channels. Crusade stories are unearthed by the reporter—the plaintiff claims maliciously. So crusade material should be viewed critically.

DOMESTIC DISCORD

Except when referring to persons with a history of domestic infelicity or to members of a set noted for the shifting of spouses, it should be assumed that a false statement of contemplated divorce or other assertion of critical domestic rift may be defamatory. In states where adultery is the only or principal ground for divorce, a false charge that Valerie was divorced by Henry may be libelous per se.

Where by statute or rule of court certain proceedings in a domestic relations court are supposed to be private in nature, there are two hazards—(i) want of the privilege which would be incident to the proceeding in open court, and (ii) contempt of court.

FINANCIAL NEWS AND COMMENT

Libel through disparagement of property is touched upon in Chapter 2. Sometimes financial writers and commentators not only disparage a business—they assert or intimate wrongful, perhaps fraudulent, conduct on the part of the corporate officers. There is no privilege when repeating the accusations and counteraccusations of a proxy fight, unless the latter is under the wing of right to reply (Chapter 9). As has been mentioned, cooperatives and charitable corporations, as well as corporations organized for profit, may be libeled. As in the case of columnists and commentators, the hazard of mistaken identity is not trivial.

JUVENILE DELINQUENTS

Reports and data concerning juvenile delinquents may not be public records. To protect the child, laws commonly authorize or require private hearings before the juvenile court. At his discretion, the judge may withhold a child's name. In such circumstances publication of a name obtained from juvenile court records or authorities may be wrongful—perhaps a contempt of court. When, however, a juvenile is formally charged in criminal court by indictment or information, there is no such restriction.

KNOW YOUR NUANCES

Chapter 2 mentions the meaning of words. If words are used precisely, there will be no opportunity for court or jury to construe language other than as intended. Is the following libel?

> The candidate for re-election is a shameless extrovert. Not only that, he practices nepotism. His only sister was once a thespian in Greenwich Village, New York. He matriculated with co-eds at the university. It is an established fact that before his marriage he habitually practiced celibacy.

The words "guilty" and "fined," for instance, refer to or at least connote a criminal procedure. Never use them when describing a civil action—in a civil action the court or jury finds for or against the defendant, and a judgment is entered.

NEW TRIALS, VERDICTS SET ASIDE, AND APPEALS

A lawsuit is not finally determined until (i) the time for an appeal has run without an appeal, or (ii) the court of final jurisdiction has spoken its final word. If the paper or newscaster has told of conviction of a crime or a finding of fraud or other obnoxious act in a civil case, a follow-up story should tell when:

> (i) the verdict is set aside or a new trial granted by the trial court; or
> (ii) the case has been reversed by the appellate court.

Otherwise a defendant (who may also resent the way the story of the trial was handled) may claim the paper did not publish a fair report of the entire proceedings.

CAUTION

Names of defendants appearing in dismissals of cases on appeal from police, traffic, and justice court convictions on motion of the prosecuting officer—thus vacating the conviction—should be checked to see if a story telling of the conviction was run. If it was, a story of the dismissal should be published. If it was not, the dismissal may be reported or ignored, depending on news value.

NO-NAME STORIES

There are two traps: (i) The person defamed may be identified despite the lack of name; or (ii) the no-name story may make difficult the use of the name in subsequent stories.

ILLUSTRATIONS

1. The headline says, "Suspect Grilled." The story says, "A clerk employed five years ago by County Treasurer Jones and dismissed last week by the present Treasurer is being questioned in connection with shortages in

the pension fund." The clerk has been identified. If not a suspect but merely a helpful witness, he has been libeled.

2. A story recites "evidence" which, to the reader, convicts an unnamed man of murder. He is arrested and charged. The paper or newscaster reports the arrest by name, carefully refraining from tie-in to the anonymous story. But the suspect can show that some people knew him to be the man referred to in the first story.

The true murderer is found and confesses. The charge against the paper's suspect is dismissed. So is the reporter.

NAME NOT ENOUGH

The *London Express* remarked that "Harold Newstead, 30 year old Camberwell man who was jailed for nine months, liked having two wives at a time." In Camberwell there were two men of about that age named Harold Newstead. The one who had not been convicted of bigamy sued the publisher. *Query:* Does the story sufficiently segregate bigamist Harold Newstead from all other Harold Newsteads by describing him as the one who served a term? What if the name had been Jones or Smith with a common first name?

"NOT" WORDS

Like "not," a number of words make mistakes easy. "Not" may be typed or set as "now." Either makes sense when read and so is easily overlooked. "He is now in jail"— or "not," which is it? When the story defames, avoid prefixes and words vulnerable to error in transmittal and printing. When using telephone or telegraph or even writing "not guilty," there is more chance of the paper printing, or the newscaster saying, "guilty" than if the copy read "acquitted" or "innocent."

OBSCENITIES AND PORNOGRAPHY

This book is not written for the edification of publishers of "girlie" magazines. But a briefest summary of the discussion of Chapter 15 may be justified. The courts have not yet reached satisfactory, stable, and workable formulas to be used when determining:

(i) whether the dominant theme (in words or pictures) appeals only to the prurient interest, or
(ii) whether, viewed as a whole, there is a literary or artistic purpose.

As a practical matter these things will be gauged by the contemporary standards of the community even though the court may speak of a "national standard." Which community? Contemporary community standards in Pine Bluff, Arkansas (where they were recently in court on this very question), may differ from those of Hollywood. Can anyone delineate a national standard comprehending both Las Vegas and a New England village with Puritan traditions not forgotten?

Some groups favor widest latitude in publishing whatever one pleases—there must be no censorship—and they claim that federal and state constitutions are on their side. Others hold to stricter standards; they assert that they are on the side of the angels.

Each publication challenged in court must be decided pretty much on its own—another instance of balancing absolute freedom of communication with other desiderata. Again—as in case of right of privacy—there will be no problem as long as John Ruskin is remembered: one of his precepts was that good taste will answer moral problems. In the field of communications, it will answer most legal dilemmas respecting charges of obscenity and pornography.

RIVALRIES—REAL AND SIMULATED

For years Jack Benny and his good friend Fred Allen helped one another by throwing brickbats at each other. Their pattern is imitated, particularly on the air, by rival phone-in (shop-talk) programs, with sideswipes at newspaper columnists or reporters and the resulting tit-for-tat from those who use the printed page. Up to a point, this is good for all concerned—many in the audience enjoy a hearty brawl. Once it gets out of hand, participants are hurt. Suits are expectable, each subject to the several defenses available against men in the public eye who attack others.

PROMISES

There is a constant temptation to place too much reliance on promises that something will happen tomorrow—the report will be filed, the suspect will be named, the officer will be dismissed. These promises are not as good as are the intentions of the men who make them because the situation may change overnight. Do not defame under the assumption that your evidence of truth will be born tomorrow. Never report a defamatory event in the past tense before that event has occurred.

SOCIETY

The society editor says such pleasant things that to her libel is almost a stranger—unless society includes a gossip column or commentator. The principal present hazard incident to the handling of social events is the expanding right of privacy cases predicated on approaching nudity in society pictures or too much prying into personal affairs, even though the words used sound friendly. See Chapter 12.

SPORTS

Sport pages and broadcasts cover more than high school and Ivy League contests. It is noticeable that since the rise of professional sports more libel cases than formerly originate in the sports room—insinuations that the goalie threw the game, or that a fighter was cowardly, are typical. Sport libel may be hard to defend; truth may be the only defense. His buddies may back the libeled player, even though before the publication they wished him off the team.

Libel suits have been brought and won by coaches, referees, race track officials, and other appendages.

WHAT LAW GOVERNS?

The writing is published or the broadcast tower situated in state A. The publication circulates or the broadcast is heard or viewed also in states B, C, D, and E. Jones, a resident of one of the latter states, is defamed. If jurisdiction over the publisher or broadcaster is obtained in the plaintiff's state, its law may apply. Or, because the dissemination of the libel was in the plaintiff's state, its laws may govern even though suit is brought in some other state. If a story goes over the wires it may be published or broadcast in every state.

SAY IT SAFELY

Wire Stories

A defamatory wire story purporting to be about a local person should not be published or broadcast unless it is checked locally to make sure as to identity and that the person named was at the place described in the story. Serious libel suits have been based upon wire stories telling of the participation of a local resident in an event occurring in a distant city when, as a matter of fact, the accused was safely at home. One wire story told of the arrest of a young woman in a "love nest" in San Francisco. It was passed along to an eager public in her home town, a thousand miles away, without being checked locally. The local girl could prove that instead of being in the love nest at the time of the arrest she had been attending church services presided over by her father, a bishop.

The court also held that there was no invasion of Senator Dodd's right of privacy. In a footnote, the opinion states:

> A threshold question, not briefed by either party and hence not decided by us, is the nature of the property right held by appellee in the contents of the files in his Senate office. Those files, themselves paid for by the United States, are maintained in an office owned by the United States, by employees of the United States. They are meant to contribute to the work of appellee as an officer of the United States. The question thus is not entirely free from doubt whether appellee has title to the contents of the files or has a right of exclusive possession of those contents, or is a bailee, or even a mere custodian of those contents.

A Supreme Court decision on this question in favor of an unauthorized publisher would strengthen the position of media in reporting on public affairs.

The caveat of the next paragraph is real but may be viewed with a rule of reason. It has to do with quoting certain types of speeches and lectures. Certainly, far more often than not, the type of utterance reported by media invites publicity. Consent to quote, as a whole or in part, is inherent in the public nature of the occasion. Indeed, the speaker yearns for maximum publicity. A fair report of what was said is safe.

Nevertheless, there may be a common law ownership of a lecture on "Memory" or "Health through Hypnotism" or what not. A lecture might be delivered as often as was "Acres of Diamonds," yet not be surrendered into the public domain and become available for printing or broadcast.

The general rule is that when, with the permission of the author or his successor, there is a general publication, the common law protection afforded literary property is lost

---

CHAPTER 18

COPYRIGHTS AND LITERARY PROPERTY

The sweat of a man's brows, and the exudations of his brains, are as much a man's own property as the breeches upon his backside.

LAURENCE STERNE

COPYRIGHT grants the author of an original work or composition in literature or the arts, and his successors, the exclusive right to multiply copies for sale. Copyrights are issued under federal statute upon publication. The federal Constitution recognizes the needs and authorizes the Congress:

> To promote the progress of science and the useful arts by securing for limited times to authors . . . the exclusive right to their respective writings . . . [Art. 1, Sec. VIII].

Prior to publication the author may have enforceable common law rights of ownership.

OWNERSHIP WITHOUT COPYRIGHT

The Federal Copyright Act provides that it shall not be construed to amend or limit the right of the author or proprietor of an unpublished work: (i) to prevent the copying, publication, or use thereof without his consent; and (ii) to recover damages if his rights be violated. Hence it is not safe to copy an uncopyrighted writing, drawing, picture, or other work unless: (i) with the provable consent of the creator or his successor as proprietor, or (ii) prior publication of the work is provable.

Within the law of defamation there may be a "publication" if the defamatory matter is communicated to one person. But it must not be assumed that a communication to one person or sometimes even to a considerable number of persons shifts the work into the public domain and makes it copyable with impunity. For example:

1. The reproduction of letters for profit is usually controlled by the writer-sender, not by the addressee. The latter may have no authority to release for publication. The author's right of privacy may also be involved. The principles of Chapter 12 would apply.
2. Delivering a manuscript for limited purposes (review, editing, or other) is not a publication.
3. The display of uncopyrighted pictures to groups is not necessarily a release into the public domain.
4. Theft of a manuscript does not terminate the rights of the lawful owner. The author of an uncopyrighted musical score would have protection even though a larcener had staged a nationwide broadcast.

Certain files of Senator Thomas J. Dodd were removed from his office at night, photocopied, and returned undamaged before the office resumed operations. Drew Pear-

son and Jack Anderson received copies of the docur knowing of their unauthorized removal. They publishe cerpts, nationwide. The holding of this important ca that Dodd could not recover damages under the theory his literary property was stolen. The Court of Appea the District of Columbia reasoned:

> . . . It has long been recognized that documents often have value above and beyond that springing from their physical possession. They may embody information or ideas whose economic value depends in part or in whole upon being kept secret. The question then arises whether the information taken by means of copying appellee's office files is of the type which the law of conversion protects.

> . . . The general rule has been that ideas or information are not subject to legal protection, but the law has developed exceptions to this rule. Where information is gathered and arranged at some cost and sold as a commodity on the market, it is properly protected as property. Where ideas are formulated with labor and inventive genius, as in the case of literary works or scientific researches, they are protected. Where they constitute instruments of fair and effective commercial competition, those who develop them may gather their fruits under the protection of the law.

> . . . The question here is not whether appellee had a right to keep his files from prying eyes, but whether the information taken from those files falls under the protection of the law of property, enforceable by a suit for conversion. In our view it does not. . . .

> . . . Insofar as we can tell, none of it amounts to literary property, to scientific invention, or to secret plans formulated by appellee for the conduct of commerce. Nor does it appear to be information held in any way for sale by appellee, analogous to the fresh news copy produced by a wire service.

Future protection stems from adherence to the requirements of the Federal Copyright Act. But there are exceptions. For example: as between rival newsgathering and publishing agencies, current news has ownership aspects. Persistent copying of news gathered by a competitor may amount to unfair competition. But the "tip" that the event has occurred may be used by anyone who makes an independent investigation and does his own composing.

BACKGROUND

The law of copyright of Western Europe can be traced back at least five hundred years. With Gutenberg the need grew.

Promptly in 1790, the Congress of the United States passed an act "for the encouragement of learning, by securing the copies of maps, charts and books to the authors and proprietors. . . ." Present law of copyright is found in (i) the Copyright Act of 1909, with some revisions; (ii) detailed rules and regulations issued under the act; and (iii) court decisions construing and enforcing the act and regulations.

Most principles applicable to literary property without copyright were developed by court decisions. In sharp contrast, copyright law is spelled out by federal statutes; the courts merely construe and enforce.

WHAT MAY BE COPYRIGHTED

A copyright is not a license to monopolize ideas and concepts. It does not give an exclusive right to report events or describe the sunset. Ordinary words and idioms as such are usable by all. Copyright has to do with phraseology, with the sequence of words and phrases, with the pictures used to express the idea, report the happening, tell the story, or advocate a cause—or with the sequence of notes used to create the tune or the rock and roll.

Copyrightable material includes nearly all original writings (except those issued by the federal government) and other creations. Illustrations are:

    (i) books, periodicals, and newspapers, or portions thereof;

    (ii) lectures and sermons;

    (iii) musical compositions and plays;

    (iv) photographs, pictorial illustrations, drawings, and cartoons;

    (v) motion pictures and television shows;

    (vi) maps, drawings, and plastic works of a scientific or technical nature;

    (vii) works of art, models, designs for works of art, and a reproduction of a work of art.

The above inventory is not all-inclusive. The act says that its enumeration shall not be held to limit the subject matter. The listing of sermons would not exclude prayers.

So if there is a desire to copy material which is not clearly in the public domain and which might be subject to copyright, it is prudent to inquire of counsel—certainly if it carries a notice of copyright.

REGISTRATION

This chapter is not concerned with how to secure or sell or bequeath a copyright or how otherwise to deal with it as proprietor. The function here is to point out when there may be violations of the rights of the proprietor.

The procedures incident to registering a copyright (with the Library of Congress) are simple. The fees are nominal.

But one should have a competent guide until the path is familiar.

DURATION—NOTICE

A copyright endures for twenty-eight years plus an extension of twenty-eight years if the author makes timely application for renewal in accordance with the act. This right to renew passes to the successors of a deceased author as defined in the act. A work first published, say, forty years ago may or may not be protected by copyright. There may have been statutory extensions which must be specifically checked in any borderline situation.

On most printed matter the minimum required notice consists of "Copyright," "Copr.," or the symbol © accompanied by the name of the proprietor and the year in which the copyright was secured. The symbol © accompanied by the initials, monogram, mark, or symbol of the proprietor puts one on notice that there may be sufficient identification elsewhere on the copy; or on its back, permanent base, or pedestal; or on the substance on which the copy is mounted.

Many publishers prefer to use a more detailed and specific notice.

A decision that a notice is insufficient and that the work is in the public domain should never be made without advice of counsel.

REVIEWS AND CRITICISM

A copyrighted work is subject to fair criticism, favorable or unfavorable, serious or humorous. To that end it may be briefly quoted and it may be described by words or pictures. But the quotations must not be of such length or the quotations and pictures so numerous that public demand to read or view the copyrighted work will be materially reduced.

The borderline between a proper review and excessive quotations (or pictures) cannot be fixed in advance by formulas applicable to all situations. If the review of the work is honestly and capably written as such, it is unlikely that either quotations or pictures will exceed permitted limits.

While criticism may be severe, the reviewer does not usually enjoy the latitude afforded critics of public affairs. See Chapter 8, "Comment and Criticism." Later we will notice other aspects of fair use.

INFRINGEMENTS

The comments and illustrations of this and the following two sections in respect to infringements apply alike to violations of common law rights of ownership before publication and infringement of a statutory copyright.

It is easy to state a general rule: any unfair appropriation of the results of the imagination, skill, and labors of the original author will constitute an offense. If the whole or a substantial part is plagiarized in the words of the original, the infringement is plain. So, too, if there is a persistent pattern of paraphrasing or variation without adequate justification. But mere similarity is not always enough. Suppose two scholars are independently engaged in historical research in a narrow field. They examine the same original documents; they read and quote many of the same old books and manuscripts. Their writings may be much the same, page after page. Yet neither has used the work of the other. Or assume that two skilled reporters cover the same event. Their stories may be very similar, though composed independently.

Another way to phrase the test is whether the one charged with the infringement has produced independently or has unfairly cribbed the product of the author. Whether there has been a violation of the rights of the proprietor depends upon the facts of and circumstances surrounding each disputed case. A choral instructor incorporated a copyrighted song in a new arrangement and had his chorus sing it. The court found an infringement. In another decision, rearrangement of a copyrighted hymn for the church choir was held a fair use. In still another case, the church itself was held liable when the choir-director-organist infringed a copyright of music.

When applying these principles, one must remember that the author will not be protected in his ideas, his theories; he will be protected in his manner of expressing them—his rhetoric and the illustrations he uses. A cartographer may copyright his map of an island; it may not be copied with impunity. Another cartographer may survey that island and produce a map almost identical; his is an independent work.

EXAMPLES OF INFRINGEMENTS

The comparison of writings, music, and other works to ascertain if there has been an infringement is often a long process. Indeed, one in-depth analysis might well consume more pages than this entire chapter. Below are listed a number of situations. They are merely markers to indicate typical danger areas.

1. An unauthorized abridgment or rearrangement of copyrighted articles from a newspaper or magazine

may be a violation. (The creation of an index may be a new work.)

2. The draftsman of an insurance policy or other legal document has no monopoly on the thought which the language expresses. But in flagrant situations of plagiarism there may be a violation.
3. Copyrighted advertising may not be used or copied.
4. The proprietor of a copyright for a musical composition has rights beyond his exclusive right to print—including a public performance for profit. Broadcasting is a public performance.
5. A member of an audience may take extensive notes and use the knowledge he has gained in his own affairs. But, without consent, he may not print and distribute or orally deliver a lecture (or other speech not already in the public domain) without the author's consent.
6. A writer of plays has wide protection but (to repeat) he cannot pre-empt exclusive control of a field of thought on a particular subject or theme.
7. Vice Admiral Rickover prepared speeches on his own time, not as a part of his official duties. He delivered them to private organizations. They had been reproduced by government facilities for purposes of security clearance and publicity. The speeches were his private property, and he was entitled to a copyright.
8. As applied to a pattern for fabrics—"graphic plagiarism" occurs when the copyist preserves the structure and important characteristics of the original design, notwithstanding systematic variation of each subordinate detail.

The similarity must be recognizable by ordinary observation. Experts may be called as witnesses. But the test is not whether hypercritical dissection reveals seeming similarities—particularly when writings are about the same event or person or subject, theory or theme. The occurrence of the same errors in two different writings is one of the most persuasive proofs of copying.

FAIR USE

An illustrative list of decisions which held there was *not* a violation (some of them "near miss" situations!) might be compiled. That would be a disservice. It might trap someone into publishing material which, under slightly changed circumstances, the court would hold to be protected.

Reviews and criticisms, already discussed, are facets of fair use. Fair use is the privilege of persons other than the copyright owner to use the material in a reasonable manner without his consent.

The doctrine of fair use is most often applied when scientific, legal, and historical materials are involved and also in connection with compilations, maps, listings, digests, and other works designed to inform. The purpose for which the use is made is of major importance. If the challenged use is for the advancement of science or the arts or knowledge generally it might well be a fair use although the same *quantum* of use for commercial purposes would be an undeniable infringement. If in doubt, secure consent; almost always it is granted readily.

As has already been indicated in another framework, a copyrighted story of a news event, published in the morning paper, may not be copied. The happening of that event, however, is a fact. The afternoon paper may send out its photographers and newsmen and create a story of its own.

LIABILITY FOR VIOLATIONS

Corporations and participating individuals are liable just about as they would be in suits based on defamation or violation of privacy. A television company is chargeable with the conduct of staff members employed to produce a broadcast script. The manager of a radio station may be personally liable just as is the editor of a newspaper. The vendor of an infringing work may be liable. So may the owner of a store who permits a concessionaire to violate copyrights. A person who employs an orchestra may be in a similar situation.

INTERNATIONAL EFFECT

Copyright laws do not have extraterritorial efficacy. However there are international conventions extending the rights that will be protected by copyright. The Berne Convention of 1886 and the Unesco Universal Copyright Convention of 1952 (effective in the United States in 1955) are the most notable. It must not be assumed that because the material was published or printed abroad it is copyable.

ACTIONABLE INFRINGEMENTS

He who claims to be the owner of the copyright cannot recover damages for a violation or stop further publication by the alleged infringer unless: (i) there has been a sufficient compliance with the provisions of the act in respect to registration, and (ii) what he registered was copyrightable. No copyright will protect the reproduction of material already in the public domain. When the requirements of registration have been met, lack of intention to infringe is usually not a defense.

The plaintiff does not have to demonstrate that the author, artist, or composer was a genius; the copyrighted material need not be strikingly unique or novel. All that is required is that the creator has done something on his own which is more than a variation from material already in the public domain.

DAMAGES—CRIMINAL SANCTIONS

It is a misdemeanor willfully and for profit to infringe a copyright or knowingly to aid or abet such infringement. Even though innocent of wrongful intent, the purloiner of another's literary property before registration or of his copyrighted property after valid registration may be required to pay damages to the owner.

TRADEMARKS

A trademark is an identification—by sign, symbol, picture, pictograph, or letters—by which the products produced or dealt in by a particular person or organization may be distinguished from those produced or dealt in by others. Absent a patent under another name, similar articles may be manufactured and sold.

The laws of many states provide for the registration of trademarks. Federal laws provide for registration of trademarks used in interstate or foreign commerce.

Copyrights, patents, and trademarks have a common element. They all stem from legal recognition of property rights derived from creative ability (of an inventor, writer, artist, composer) or from quality in performance—a good product, year after year. Day after day the literary production of a columnist could be copyrighted. If he regularly uses a certain distinctive headline, that may be registered as a trademark.

As noted in illustrations already given, a label with at least a modicum of artistic merit and ingenuity may be copyrighted. Within it or within an advertisement may be a trademark—registered as such and also used separately.

Like copyrights, patents are not of indefinite duration. If

a man ingeniously makes a grandfather's clock, he and his successors will own it forever. But if he invents a device to make all clocks better, he and his successors will own the invention no longer than the statutory period.

CONGRESSIONAL CAVEAT

For many years there have been rumblings of coming Congressional changes in the statutory law in respect to copyrights. It is to be "modernized."

So if you read or hear of new federal law pertaining to copyrights, be sure to consult your attorney before accepting the statements of this chapter in respect to statutory law as gospel. Or check with your attorney to be sure there have been no statutory changes.

Meanwhile be chary of excessive use of photocopy machines, particularly when you make multiple copies of important segments of a book or of an article.

CHAPTER 19

THE FEDERAL
CONSTITUTION

One country, one constitution, one destiny.

DANIEL WEBSTER

. . . The most remarkable work known to me in modern times to have been produced by the human intellect.

WILLIAM EWART GLADSTONE

THE objective of this chapter is to inventory for ready reference the constitutional provisions most frequently involved in current stories, comments, and editorials.

There is no attempt to discuss the Constitution as a whole. It was framed by the Constitutional Convention held in Philadelphia in 1787 and was adopted by the requisite number of states (nine) in 1789. No one can state its purposes better or more succinctly than does the Preamble:

WE THE PEOPLE of the United States, in Order to form a more perfect Union, establish Justice, insure domestic

Tranquility, provide for the common defence, promote
the general Welfare, and secure the Blessings of Liberty
to ourselves and our Posterity, do ordain and establish
this Constitution for the United States of America.

The first ten amendments, packaged as the Bill of Rights,
were adopted December 15, 1791. They follow immediately after the Constitution.

Here we will quote or digest, with briefest comment:
Section 8 of Article I which grants powers to Congress, the
six articles of the Bill of Rights which most often appear in
news or comment, and five later amendments which seem
to be of particular interest to the Fourth Estate.

Congress is accorded seventeen powers, ranging from finance (including the coining of money) and taxation, to constituting "Tribunals inferior to the supreme Court," patents
and copyrights, "Post Offices and post Roads," and the mili-
tary establishment. Foresightedly, Congress was granted
authority:

To define and punish Piracies and Felonies committed on
the high Seas, and Offenses against the Law of Nations.

The listing of legislative powers ends with an omnibus:

To make all Laws which shall be necessary and proper for
carrying into Execution the foregoing Powers, and all
other Powers vested by this Constitution in the Government of the United States, or in any Department or
Officer thereof.

But the above quoted blanket paragraph is seasoned by the
Tenth Amendment which reads:

The powers not delegated to the United States by the
Constitution, nor prohibited by it to the States, are reserved to the States respectively, or to the people.

So despite the proliferation of bureaus and federal activities, the constitutional *theory* is that the federal government is one of limited powers.

THE BILL OF RIGHTS

Six of the first ten amendments often appear in news stories, comments, and editorials. *The First Amendment* (they are called "articles" in formal parlance) is the shibboleth of all who deal in news and public affairs. So familiar is it that it seems scarcely necessary to quote:

> Congress shall make no law respecting an establishment of religion, or prohibiting the free exercise thereof; or abridging the freedom of speech, or of the press, or the right of the people peaceably to assembly, and to petition the Government for a redress of grievances.

This amendment is primary in protecting media from governmental control. The Supreme Court has said the selection of copy for publication "whether fair or unfair—constitutes the exercise of editorial control and judgment. It has yet to be demonstrated how government regulations of this crucial process can be exercised consistently with First Amendment guarantees of a free press." (Users of the people's airwaves are in a somewhat different category.)

The Fourth Amendment: The Fourth Amendment assures:

> The right of the people to be secure in their persons, houses, papers, and effects, against unreasonable searches and seizures, shall not be violated, and no Warrants shall issue, but upon probable cause, supported by Oath or affirmation, and particularly describing the place to be searched, and the persons or things to be seized.

SAY IT SAFELY

Some law enforcement officials say that this amendment is a shield to those who break the law. The courts are forever struggling with cases where the accused claims rights under it. Reporters write stories of the encounters. There is an impact on the right of privacy.

The Fifth Amendment: The Fifth Amendment covers wide ranges:

> No person shall be held to answer for a capital, or otherwise infamous crime, unless on a presentment or indictment of a Grand Jury, except in cases arising in the land or naval forces, or in the Militia, when in actual service in time of War or public danger; nor shall any person be subject for the same offence to be twice put in jeopardy of life or limb, nor shall be compelled in any criminal case to be a witness against himself, nor be deprived of life, liberty, or property, without due process of law; nor shall private property be taken for public use without just compensation.

Here we find the ubiquitous "due process of law" provision. Its impact is present in many stories.

The Sixth Amendment: This amendment also safeguards those accused of crime. There shall be a speedy and public trial by an impartial jury. The accused shall be informed of the nature and cause of the accusation. Secret testimony is proscribed. Accused is accorded the right to be confronted with the witnesses against him. He can compel the attendance of witnesses in his favor. He is entitled to have the assistance of counsel for his defense.

During the last decade this amendment has been the foundation stone for public-defender establishments, much in the news.

The Seventh Amendment: The right of trial by jury in

civil cases is preserved. Its verdict may not be reexamined except according to the rules of the common law.

The amendment does not mandate a jury trial in *all* civil cases.

The Eighth Amendment: This amendment is in the forefront of current news:

> Excessive bail shall not be required, nor excessive fines imposed, nor cruel and unusual punishments inflicted.

Is all capital punishment cruel *and* unusual? The draftsmen of the Constitution were writing in 1787.

Presently media are confronted with much debate as to the fairness and effectiveness of governmental machinery pertaining to the enforcement of crime. The courts are a part, but only a part, of it. The prosecutor and the law enforcement officers bring the cases to court.

Nearly two hundred years ago the writers of the Bill of Rights seemed as much concerned about criminal justice as are we today.

SOME SUBSEQUENT AMENDMENTS

The oft quoted Fourteenth Amendment (adopted July 28, 1868) is frequently credited with freeing the slaves. That was done nearly three years earlier by the *Thirteenth Amendment:*

> 1. Neither slavery nor involuntary servitude, except as a punishment for crime whereof the party shall have been duly convicted, shall exist within the United States, or any place subject to their jurisdiction.
> 2. Congress shall have power to enforce this article by appropriate legislation.

The Fourteenth Amendment: This is the longest of all the amendments, divided into five paragraphs. The vital due process of law and equal protection of the law clauses are found in the first paragraph:

> 1. All persons born or naturalized in the United States, and subject to the jurisdiction thereof, are citizens of the United States and of the State wherein they reside. No State shall make or enforce any law which shall abridge the privileges or immunities of citizens of the United States; nor shall any State deprive any person of life, liberty, or property, without due process of law, nor deny to any person within its jurisdiction the equal protection of the laws.

Paragraph two has to do with the apportionment of representatives, elections, and related matters. Paragraph three is concerned with the eligibility for public office of persons who have engaged in rebellion against the United States. Paragraph four faces the public debt.

The concluding fifth paragraph gives powers to Congress to the end that the Fourteenth Amendment may be enforced:

> 5. The Congress shall have power to enforce by appropriate legislation the provisions of this article.

The Supreme Court has decided that the Fourteenth Amendment makes the Bill of Rights applicable to state governments. Obviously, in 1791 the amendments constituting the Bill of Rights were adopted as protection against the encroachments of the then newly organized federal government.

The Fifteenth Amendment: Adopted March 30, 1870, this amendment made certain that the right of a citizen to vote shall not be denied or abridged "on account of race, color, or previous condition of servitude." The states are specifically included. Again Congress is given power to enforce.

The Sixteenth Amendment: On February 25, 1913, Congress was given "power to lay and collect taxes on incomes." Proposed amendments to put a ceiling on rates were voted down because, it was argued, no one could imagine rates exceeding ten percent; ergo, a limitation was unnecessary.

The Eighteenth Amendment (January 29, 1919) was the Noble Experiment and *the Twenty-first Amendment* (December 5, 1933) repealed it.

The Nineteenth Amendment (August 26, 1920): The right to vote "shall not be denied or abridged" on account of sex. Made applicable to the states, Congress was given power to enforce.

The Twenty-fourth Amendment (February 4, 1964): Poll taxes as prerequisite to the right to vote in federal elections were forbidden.

The foregoing references to constitutional provisions do not carry an implication that they are necessarily the most important provisions of the Constitution. Whatever provision is before the court is the most important provision *for that case.* As stated at the beginning, in this chapter we have but tried to list, for ready reference, the provisions most likely to be involved in the news and in public debate.

CHAPTER 20

THIRTY

The great end of life is not knowledge but action.

T. H. HUXLEY

NATURAL questions are: In the field of communications is the law becoming more or less strict? Are handcuffs being put upon the wrists of publishers? Looking only to fundamentals, there are two answers. At first glance they seem inconsistent, but actually they are not.

When performing the vital functions of scrutinizing, reporting, and commenting upon public affairs, media are afforded greater protection than was formerly available to shield them.

When publicizing purely personal and private affairs, media are now held to higher standards of accuracy and consideration than in years past. The extension of protection to persons not in the public eye flows mainly through the channel of the right of privacy.

We have but described the high spots—perhaps not all of them. Nevertheless, study and periodic reading of the rules here given will enable anyone dealing with writings, pictures, or broadcasting to recognize the danger signals.

Possible libel having been recognized, a story or editorial satisfactory to all but the most ardent propagandist can be produced without appreciable risk (or, at least, without undue risk) in almost every situation.

Like a chart, this book notes the rocks and shallows and shows the aids to navigation. Vast areas of clear sailing are unmentioned. There is plenty of room to maneuver stories and editorials and to publish and broadcast pictures if a wary eye is kept on the markers here listed. As emphasized in Chapter 1, because this is a danger signal manual, *in close cases the law has been stated in stricter terms than the court should enforce.* Sometimes exceptions to and variations of the rules here given will be sufficient legal answer if a publication or broadcast is questioned in court. But to go into them in this book would be a disservice to the men and women for whom it is written.

Often it is difficult to defend a libel suit. Just as often it is difficult for the plaintiff to win—particularly when the plaintiff's past is shady and it is clear that the publisher or broadcaster was careful and the mistake natural, hence perhaps excusable. Jurymen, too, have erasers on their pencils.

Most rules of law are subject to exceptions. This is especially so in the field of libel. There the law must permit actual injury to be done without redress; novel and involved principles are brought into play. There has been no attempt to write a legal treatise, suitable for use by lawyers or a judge. Because every month brings fresh decisions from the court, a book purporting to delve into every detail would be outmoded before it was off the press.

The objective here has been to state the basic rules in simple terms and to show how they apply to typical situations. Except when the preceding pages have given express or implicit warning of the hazards of local idiosyncrasies, these fundamental principles and concepts should be adequate guideposts.

If, by inviting closer collaboration with counsel, we have persuaded the publisher to seek advice in advance, we shall have made a great contribution to pocketbooks as well as to peace of mind. An attorney is inexpensive when consulted in advance, relatively costly when called in after the event. One of the purposes of this book is to promote a sixth sense as to when counsel should be called.

THE RIGHT TO KNOW

Because freedom of the press is taken for granted in this country, it is easy to forget that (i) the right is relatively new; (ii) in many lands it does not exist; and (iii) there are forces which would undermine it here. An eminent American historian remarked, "We need, from time to time, to take a look at the things that go without saying to see if they are still going."

Freedom of the press and freedom of speech were written into the federal Constitution at a time when there were no such freedoms in England. Two decades after the adoption of our Constitution, an English publisher was convicted of crime because he criticized Parliament.

As was stated in the introduction and as, we hope, is implicit throughout, the purpose of this manual is not to frighten publishers and broadcasters into saying less. It is to help them be secure in saying what should be said. Many a bureaucrat, in Washington, in state capitals, in the city hall, and in the county courthouse, would prefer that the news touching governmental affairs be limited to mimeographed handouts. The premise of this book is that, except where national security is actually involved, the citizens of this country have a right to know what is going on. Unless they do, the country will not long preserve its relative freedom.

Early in the book it was mentioned that, when used here, the words "publisher," "publish," and "publishing" are words of art referring to the communication of the defamation, however, communicated. They include the writer of a letter as well as all persons involved in the production, printing, and (possibly) circulation of a newspaper, magazine, book, or circular. They include cameramen, processors, commentators, and everyone who participates in putting the defamatory broadcast on the air, as well as the owner of the station. They include the person who displays a statue as well as the sculptor and the institution which exhibits a defamatory picture as well as the artist.

In short—all those who communicate in any fashion are included. Their messages can be fully as effective, arouse fewer antagonisms, and be more profitable if said safely.

INDEX

235

INDEX

INDEX

MILLS COLLEGE LIBRARY

BNF   Say it safely : legal limits in pu
345.73 A826s 1976   Ashley, Paul Pritcha

3 3086 00014 2687

345.73   A826s
                                          1976

Mills College Library
Withdrawn

MILLS COLLEGE
LIBRARY